JEAN SANS TERRE

JEAN SANS TERRE

by YVAN GOLL

preface by W. H. AUDEN

drawings by EUGENE BERMAN

MARC CHAGALL

SALVADOR DALI

New York · THOMAS YOSELOFF · *London*

critical notes by **LOUISE BOGAN**

CLARK MILLS

JULES ROMAINS

ALLEN TATE

translations of the Poems by

LIONEL ABEL · LÉONIE ADAMS · JOHN PEALE BISHOP ·
LOUISE BOGAN · BABETTE DEUTSCH · JOHN GOULD FLETCHER
· ISABELLA GARDNER · CLAIRE AND YVAN GOLL · PAUL
GOODMAN · GALWAY KINNELL · W. S. MERWIN · CLARK MILLS ·
ROBERT NURENBERG · KENNETH PATCHEN · GEORGE REAVEY
· KENNETH REXROTH · ERIC SELLIN · WILLIAM JAY
SMITH · ROBERT WERNICK · WILLIAM CARLOS WILLIAMS

THOMAS YOSELOFF, PUBLISHER
11 EAST 36TH STREET
NEW YORK 16, N. Y

THOMAS YOSELOFF LTD.
123 NEW BOND STREET
LONDON W. 1, ENGLAND

PRINTED IN THE UNITED STATES OF AMERICA
AMERICAN BOOK—STRATFORD PRESS, INC., NEW YORK

Preface

To pass judgment on poetry written in another tongue than one's own is impudent and I shall not attempt to evaluate Yvan Goll as a poet. The translation of poetry is so difficult and thankless a task that no one, unless he greatly loves and admires a poem, will think of attempting it: the distinguished list of translators of *Jean Sans Terre* testifies to the esteem in which the author is held by his Anglo-American colleagues.

Judgment is impossible, but even literary *placement* is dangerous. I can safely say, I think, that one of M. Goll's poetic ancestors is the Rimbaud of *Bateau Ivre* and *Une Saison en Enfer* because there is almost no contemporary French poetry, and little modern poetry anywhere, which Rimbaud has not influenced, but should I try to be more specific to decide for example whether Yvan Goll is or is not a surrealist,

I should find myself in the position of a historian who would discuss fourth-century Christianity without knowing the difference between *homo-ousios* and *homoi-ousios*.

One is left, therefore, with what can only, though most inadequately, be called subject matter. Whatever language they may write in, all poets living in the same historical period and more or less the same kind of society answer such questions as "What experiences are important and authentic? What is a good, what is a bad man? What is man's relation to Nature, his neighbors, the past and the future?" in ways which, despite all differences, are more like the answers of their predecessors.

Thus the hero of M. Goll's cycle of poems, Jean Sans Terre, or John Landless, is an Everyman figure, but a very different Everyman from the hero of the medieval morality play. Like the Quest Hero of fairy tales he takes journeys, but these journeys are of another kind. Spenser and Goll both make use of dreams and dream imagery, but there the resemblance ends.

It would be interesting some time to make a historical study of the notion of Everyman and of his literary treatment. The Classical world, for example, lacked him; it knew only the exceptional man, the epic or tragic hero, and the chorus of citizens who keep the Golden Mean.

Everyman first appears in Christendom as an expression of the belief that every soul is equally the child of God, and his true end, even if he refuse it, to become a citizen of the Heavenly city. During the Renaissance we hear very little about him, but he returns in the age of the Enlightenment as the Man of Common Sense, a citizen of the universal city of Reason.

During the early period, at least, of Romanticism, he disappears again in favor of the heroic Faustian explorer of new experiences, of the Byronic rebel against unjust and outworn conventions. With the full development of technology he has reappeared as the Collective Man and grown so big that he now elbows almost every other figure off the scene. There have been few more revolutionary changes in human sensibility than that which, after the first World War, made all

6

countries, victors and vanquished alike, erect monuments, not to great commanders, but to the Unknown Soldier or, as Yvan Goll would call him, Landless John.

To own land signifies membership in some particular *polis*, with its particular memories, traditions, beliefs, ways of living. But the Machine has destroyed every such *polis*; it has made all lands its land, reduced all ways of living to its single way. Worse still, having deprived us of personal experience, it submerges us in a flood of arbitrary unfelt facts. Think of the amount of information contained in one issue of a Sunday newspaper; think of the radio—five minutes of Old Dutch music, five minutes of recipes followed by a talk on Buddhism or some primitive tribe in New Guinea, etc.

Surrealism seems a very natural response to a world in which our daily life comes more and more to resemble a dream, in which we must passively submit to a succession of incongruous and discontinuous experiences.

Jean Sans Terre is equally at home on the Ponte Vecchio and Brooklyn Bridge because neither is really his: he must sleep on "the mattress of the thousand truths" because he is personally committed to none. Cut off from a personal past ("The King is dead, I'm not his heir"), estranged from Nature ("The sea-gulls all their patience gone/Head for another universe"), and confined to suburbs where "The insane trees drink petrol," no longer anyone in particular ("Wifeless with nothing"), he has become, fantastically, everybody and everything:

> He crosses the bridges of all the ages
> The bridges of all contradictions
> From the left bank to the right bank
> From yes to no from just to unjust

He is the Wandering Jew, forced to be forever on the move without any hope of finding hidden treasure or a Sleeping Beauty, without even the Whitmanesque exhilaration of the novelty of the Open Road, forever anxious about a future which he cannot imagine:

7

He asks the mirror if he will arrive on time
On time no matter where nowhere

Of course, with the loss of his past, certain evils are buried, such as the intolerance of his forefathers who "used the oaks to hang a man with thoughts," but neither he nor, I fancy, Yvan Goll, take much comfort from that. One would not say that Jean Sans Terre, any more than the rest of us, was a strikingly happy man.

W. H. AUDEN

Contents

11

Critical Notes

I

In pre-Romantic periods, man is nothing; it is his terrors
that count. Poetry's long stay in the region of pre-Romanti-
cism is the oddest phenomenon in the literature of our day.
Dada and Surrealism announced themselves as an end, re-
fusing to look forward to any further development beyond
itself. The poets of Surrealism remained singularly naïve con-
cerning the atmosphere they created, and considered themselves "new"—without forerunners or historic exemplars. It
is becoming clear, however, that in Surrealism—its delight in
the horrorweighted scene, the dark region, and the grisly
fetish—the whole macabre of pre-Romantic Gothic has made
another appearance. The haunted silent squares and arcades

of Chirico, rather than the haunted castle of Radcliffe, set the stage. And the "subconscious" imagery of Surrealist poetry corresponds to the subconscious imagery of Blake, Young and Poe. In both periods, as an escape from harsh reality, poetry recedes back to the play and the primitive terrors of the savage and the child.

But there are signs that the spell is about to be broken. Yvan Goll says of his *Jean Sans Terre*:

> Renouant la tradition du Romantisme, Jean Sans Terre, ne craint pas de fêter de nouvelles noces avec la Lune, avec la Nature tout entière . . . Surréalisme avait refoulé la Nature à l'office, comme servante du prétentieux Moi humain . . . Dans Jean Sans Terre la Nature redevient sujet principal. Cependant elle n'apparait plus à l'état brut, mais soumise aux procédés scientifiques de l'époque moderne. Ce qui n'empêche pas l'homme de l'adorer d'une façon toute païenne, comme dans les temps antiques . . .

In these words an actual Romantic spirit and feeling reappears. The secularized Flesh and Devil have been surpassed and passed beyond. Now actual Nature comes back for applause. The stage sets, the underground corridors, the deserted public squares with their frozen shadows, the blank shores with empty horizons, yield to recognizable landscapes. And emotion, no longer disguised and transformed, returns freshly and without shame; and can be applied directly to the earth, the sun, moon and stars, to animals and flowers, and to man. Although the atmosphere of displacement, of nostalgia, is still very strong, man is released from full helplessness before the childish dream. He is no longer completely at the mercy of events. He is free of the full burden of his situation, because he is now free to apply to it both irony and love.

This is the Romantic spirit at its best, and in Yvan Goll's *Jean Sans Terre*, it is always evident. The poet creates, as well, in the best Romantic tradition, a myth which will accommodate all the capabilities of a sensitive and complex observer. The Romantic Character often embodies itself in some one figure (such as the Byronic Don Juan and Childe

Harold): or in two complementary figures (Faust-Mephisto). Jean Sans Terre is such a romantic embodiment. The modern mythical personage, however, is never a "hero." The "I" has been subdued; the action becomes more metaphysical than physical; the "adventures" are more the movements of the spirit than of the body.

The poet is turned toward the actual world. He observes, and lays himself open to emotion; he does not create a phantasmagoria in which he can only suffer and feel frustration. He looks upon a world, from the calm and lucidity of his self, which, it is true, presents all the characteristics of the nightmare, but he is not for a moment subdued or taken in by it. Jean Sans Terre becomes not only a picture of the guiltless Jew dispossessed, but of the man of any race, equipped with the most modern sensitiveness, thrown into a world in which there are no values and little love; where suspicion and hatred come more easily than understanding and tolerance; where the non-conforming individual can find no place; where materialism will yield only to forces as limited, brutal and harsh as itself. Yvan Goll has created a character that combines medieval mysticism with an observation modern in the extreme. The two faculties are applied to all aspects of our times. Jean Sans Terre explores the modern city as well as the modern relationship between man and woman, between the dream and the dreamer, between "God" and the pitiable human machine, made of dust but housing the idea of the universe.

Jean Sans Terre, in the three volumes already published in France, is epically conceived. Yvan Goll has not, however, burdened his conception with epic treatment. He comes before us, this John Landless, presented by a lyric poet: a lyricist skilled in special effects of technique and language. M. Goll has been able to use the brilliant Surrealist vocabulary, while charging and weighting it in a manner unknown to Surrealism. He has gone beyond Apollinaire in making the "popular" form serve as vehicle for philosophical and metaphysical ideas. He has perfected an instrument which, at first glance, seems slight, and has given it, by a dazzling mastery over effects, true depth and range.

Louise Bogan

II

If we consider the long poems written in French or English during the past forty years, they seem to share one weakness in common—this is the absence of any central core, or armature, sufficiently solid to force the poem into an organic whole, and fertile enough to provide wealth of idea and symbol. This armature may take any one of innumerable forms; it is present in every long poem, or group of related poems, we preserve for its whole excellence. It may adopt the form of an inanimate object (*The Bridge*, of Hart Crane); an abstract concept (the city, in Verhaeren or Romains); a word used as symbol, the reality of which the poet does not know from experience (the sea, in Rimbaud's *Bateau Ivre*); an opposition between ideas (the ever-present Christian doctrine of spirit and flesh, ideal and real, in almost all Baudelaire's poems); it may be anything the poet likes, an old or new legend or myth, or any temporary *idée fixe*; it is related to the finished work more intimately than the spinal cord to the body; it holds the form in position and, in a sense, creates the parts.

The series of poems entitled *Jean Sans Terre* by Yvan Goll is one of the few poems in any language, certainly the only poem in French, which can be said to possess such an armature, which is Jean himself, citizen of the world, and mirror of contemporary man. *Jean Sans Terre* is an epic poem, in which the central character is not, as in the past, a hero or a man of action—today such men are their own spokesmen—nor even the king, John Lackland; but simply the individual, perfectly conscious of the world and of his place in it, and yet powerless to change the fate either of his species or of himself. He is timely in that his problems spring from our world of refugees, fallen systems and hierarchies, and universal war; he is timeless in that his enthusiasm, sufferings and potentialities are simple, and are those of all men at all moments of history.

In the character of Jean, who is landless and a great traveler, having made in the first poem in the series "a sevenfold voyage into the world," there are obvious similarities with other legends risen from many times and places; he recalls Don Juan, Childe Harold, the Wandering Jew, Peter Schlemihl, and even the Chaplin familiar to Europeans; he is distantly related to the troubadours, and evokes the beggardom, the mysteries, the *jeux*, the *dits*, the *rondels* and the *fabliaux* of a medieval Bohemia.

The epithet "landless" lends itself to all interpretations. It describes more than a man without a country, a man divorced from the land and all that the land signifies, particularly to the French, from peasant to nobility. (A man's title, his mark of identity, the name of a piece of land.) Divorced from the land, he is divorced automatically from provincial traditions and customs, from property, the possession of things, and therefore from conformity, the irrevocable law of possession.

Thus the negative "landless" rests on Jean not as a burden and misfortune—though often it seems these, even to him—but as a visible token of his freedom from the constraints and intangible burdens his fellows create more than willingly. Belonging to no village, no region, no class, no continent, he can absorb all forms of experience, all cultures. He is available; he can abandon himself to a given milieu. A member of no movement or institution, he is part of them all; landless, he inherits the earth.

But freedom exacts payment in responsibilities and difficulties; and as freedom approaches the absolute, as with Jean, the cost increases in proportion. On the summits Jean is at times afforded visions of grandeur and glimpses of immense perspectives; but at others he cannot escape his own pitiless self-judgment, his vicarious suffering for others not landless, and above all the terrors and desires that take form in his solitude.

From the revelation to silence, from the depths to the heights, and back, he moves like a pendulum; by turns nostalgic, triumphant, elegiac and in despair, but always volatile, he explores himself and his milieus; and the record of his discoveries is, simply, an account of his life and our own.

The majority of the poems of Jean Sans Terre are written in the most rigid and mechanically difficult pattern that exists in French: the rhymed quatuaron and the five-syllable line. In adopting this despotic form, Goll has forced his expressions to inhabit the smallest possible space. The form in the earlier poems seems to have hypnotized him, happily, so that at times his thought seems intensified to the point of a violent explosion. This effect has not often been attained in French poetry; we find it certainly in Rimbaud's *Bateau Ivre*, in separate lines in Baudelaire, and in a few lyrics by Apollinaire; but scarcely anywhere else.

In his later poems—"Jean Sans Terre Crosses the Atlantic," "Jean Sans Terre Discovers the West Pole," and the others— Goll has abandoned this short form, moving through the alexandrine toward freer verbal patterns, which may in the future become more rhythmic than metrical, and be marked by an increased subtlety in the use of internal rhyme.

But in all the poems, early and late, Goll has shown himself to be a virtuoso in the use of language. The highly elaborated verbal patterns, the subtlety and multiplicity of meanings, the linked and interlocking chains of associations, create effects we may greet with envy and delight. In contact with one another, word, idea and symbol create vibrations, which associate in their turn with others more material, risen from the sounds themselves, producing harmonies which elude analysis. In this Goll has managed to profit by the advantages of the Surrealist method—freedom of the imagination, and brilliance of verbal texture, without succumbing to its weaknesses—and has produced poetry which suggests music and yet says what it means.

In *Jean Sans Terre*, then, Yvan Goll has recognized the

dilemmas and complexities of his time; through a rigorous selection he has managed to isolate a large number of the basic elements and themes, timely and timeless, which run through our lives like ore through seams of rock; gradually, from poem to poem, he has achieved a perceptual and sympathetic scope and depth equaled by no French poet now living, and comparable with Rimbaud and Baudelaire. Finally, in the character of Jean Sans Terre, he has created a legend capable of supporting not only the poems now written but also the others to come.

Whatever the future adventures and sufferings of Jean Sans Terre, whether he rounds the earth one more time or simply drops off to sleep, his life is ours, and is filled with a wary confidence in the future of individual man.

Clark Mills

III

The first half of the twentieth century has been a difficult period for poetry, in France as everywhere.

The causes lie in many places: in the recent history of poetry itself, the troubled spirit of the times in general, and the increasingly insubstantial and arachnidean character of the relations between man and poetry.

The evil afflicting poetry is expressed in the growth—still going on—of various inhibitions, timidity and paralyzing modesty, which are not without analogy in the field of painting.

Someday this strange misfortune will be studied, elucidated, and perhaps rectified—provided civilization does not collapse, and the dizziness of our mechanical acceleration leaves us capable of reflection on such subjects. When this happens, a few exceptional figures will emerge into new prominence, some because they will have been vigorous enough to cross this deadly climate unscathed, and others—still subtler victory—because they will have discovered on the way edible fruits of surprising flavor, oases and outcroppings of eternal poetry.

Yvan Goll belongs to the second category, along with two or three others, such as Léon-Paul Fargue.

Already the man himself was unforgettable. When I think of him, I see, moving out of the shadows, a being fine and vibrant as a diapason. Also I see his eyes, which looked as if they were made to radiate light, gentleness, and a kind of brotherly disenchantment.

Yvan Goll has given us the epic of *Jean Sans Terre*, which brings to mind on the one hand the *Grand Testament* of Villon, and on the other hand Heinrich Heine's *Lieder*. Indeed, of the modern European writers, it is Heine that he resembles most. He shows the same poignant sweetness and tender irony. Like Heine as well, Yvan Goll is the product of the meeting and intermingling of two traditions, of two poetic veins, the German and the French.

In this connection, Yvan Goll also reminds us of Gérard de Nerval, whose ability to relate other-worldliness and everyday reality in an easy, natural manner is the quality I like so much in his work.

Jean Sans Terre, after having been for Yvan Goll merely an occasional personage in his interior theater—a representative only slightly more privileged than Verlaine's Gaspard Hauser—became his principal character and delegate, armed with full powers of expression and in charge of all his relations with the world.

The case is more unusual than one would suppose, and it brings about considerable changes in the lyric attitude. Other poets have created heroes who were their doubles, the projections of their other selves in space. But I think none has done it with such faithfulness and continuous growth as Yvan Goll.

It is a mistake to think of this as a merely formal device. In spite of the many resemblances to the self and the self's messages which he bears, the hero is separate from the self and is no longer the person who uses the word "I." He takes root in the universe around him. He acquires three dimensions, instead of being only the poet's exhalation or his subjective exclamation. He moves in a different light, assumes poses or postures which surprise the poet, who would not have perceived their strange, pathetic, or bizarre qualities had he been using the word "I."

From this, in particular, springs a kind of humor which a purely subjective attitude cannot equal. As long as subjectivity prevails, the self may become the subject matter of its own humor only at the expense of contortions which betray this subjectivity and strain.

It is this, for example, which makes Laforgue's poetry seem labored and affected.

As an experiment, reread the *Jean Sans Terre* poems you like best, the ones you find most moving.

Imagine "Jean" replaced by "I." The tone will change. The charm, the emotion, will remain perhaps, but their color and persuasive force will be surprisingly different.

Yvan Goll, however, by this projection of himself into the outside world, has found the means to say everything which was essential in what he had to say. It will not be difficult for future commentators to decipher the autobiographical confession. One finds in the poems sometimes the real events of his life, sometimes the dreamed or wished-for events, sometimes the chief features of his own character. In certain cases this autobiographical interpretation will be made easier by the existence of successive versions of the same poem. One can locate the changes and examine the sediment, often extremely fine and transparent, which experience has deposited.

The chronology of these poems is of great interest to the student of poetry (and I wish it were possible to include a list of the dates of composition). For it reveals Yvan Goll's double progress: toward the richness of what he had to say and toward assurance in his means of saying it.

I would add willingly: toward the use of certain rhythms. But it is not clear that he chose these rhythms deliberately. More likely they are the result of happy encounters and the influence which a successful technique, once hit upon and experienced, exercises thereafter on the hand of the artist.

I believe I am right in thinking that the poems of Yvan Goll which are most accomplished and unforgettable are those which are written in stanzas consisting of four short lines, in an unvarying meter of up to eight feet per line.

In five-foot lines, however, the poet is most at home and most visibly satisfied. In the five-foot line he recreates best Jean Sans Terre's persistent, patient, interminable march and makes of his footsteps, of that rapping on always alien soil, an obsession in our memory.

The images should be discussed at length. Recent poetry has made us unaccustomed to such effectiveness and necessity, but left us nostalgic for them.

Yvan Goll never confused the superficial language of the intellect with the dictates of the soul, nor mistook words pulled out of a hat for the incalculable flashing forth of the word.

JULES ROMAINS
[Translated by GALWAY KINNELL]

IV

These poems must be read all together because they are one poem. Only then will the reader begin to understand the depth and range of Yvan Goll's powers of invention.

The man without a country is hardly a new figure. But Jean Sans Terre becomes more than the exile: not only is he the exile who does not have a country; there are no longer countries. Yvan Goll with the instinct of a real poet has taken a common symbol and pushed it further than anybody else before him. Jean Sans Terre is the man without a world.

This poet is a refugee but that only adds to the immediate interest of his hero without in any sense creating it. Landless John—I could not persuade Mr. Goll to call him John Landless, which putting his condition into his surname would to my mind render it in its full pathos—John has been tossed up on the surface of life by the tensions and anxieties of French society in the thirties. Yet if he were merely a social and political figure he would lose most of the very real interest that he has. I confess that my own interest in these poems—an interest which I felt before I saw their merit as poetry—was stirred by certain similarities between Yvan Goll's view of modern man and my own.

Jean Sans Terre is the man without history; but as a literary symbol he has been known in the past, and is part of our literary history. I say this not to detract from Yvan Goll's originality, but actually to praise it: his symbolic wanderer is not a private fiction, he is based solidly upon an experience that began to be known a hundred years ago. Gérard de Nerval, Baudelaire, and Rimbaud would have understood him. Yvan Goll's contribution to this tradition is that he has understood him in a new way.

The translations of *Jean Sans Terre* are of uneven merit, but the best ones will give the American without French a fair idea of Yvan Goll's rapid pace and command of imagery. For instance the poem "Jean Sans Terre and His Shadow" would prove to any good reader that Yvan Goll is not merely a poet of "crisis," but is able to extend his immediate symbol into one of the great modes of poetry.

ALLEN TATE

JEAN SANS TERRE

IDENTITY OF JEAN SANS TERRE

Tantalus' son wrong from the start
In orchards of men I went unfed
Blank looks froze my flaming heart
The only loves I tasted fled

I walked the Street of Seven Sorrows
Went down the stairs the servants use
And passed the bridges of the Styx
The waiting rooms, the subterrainbows

I was the guest with a sad face
Innkeepers gave me a wide berth
My wine left bloodstains at my place
My shadows soiled the virgin earth

I slept among veronicas
Sucked eggs of nightingales at night
Butchered the magic unicorn
Ate birds but could not digest their flight

And landless still, after long forage:
Of the dead King I am not heir
The fruit on the Tree of Knowledge
Has spoiled; and I am hungrier

I will have been brief as the foam
On the crest of breakers afloat—
Born starless in the moonless gloom
My name but a catch in the throat

[*Translated* *by* GALWAY KINNELL]

JEAN SANS TERRE
THE DOUBLE MAN

I am the Unique and the Double Being
The King of Hearts upright and reversed
Losing winning passed passer-by day in death out
I am the Self and soon my memory

I am the Moment and its double message
Although my right bank does not know the left
In my name East and West elope
I am the nuptials of the Yes and No

The river flows down twice: you see his soul and body
Dip in your hand and you caress the cloud
The moon blooms at the seaweed branches
Fish waves its fins through globes of fire

I am the man with twin shores. I'm the man
Of two profiles: the assassin the saint
My hero-Chest may hide a coward's neck
My male flank yields to my female breasts

Right hand: what have you done with your left hand?
Between the rose of dawn and the rust of dusk
The river does he judge? Blind river flows
Weary to immortality

From the bank of flesh to the bank of mind
Time throws its slow wave unsubdued
I am the King of Hearts passed passer-by
Gambler on both sides: I must win—death!

[*Translated by* JOHN GOULD FLETCHER]

Drawing by Eugene Berman

JEAN SANS TERRE
AND HIS SHADOW

(First Version)

Shadow! Fraternal shadow
Moving with me lying at ease
In candlelight and the light of day
Inevitable Siamese

Must I love you as a brother
Fruit of the same womb unknown
Or despise you as another
Grimace of the hunchback devil shown?

Following Saturnian river-banks
You brush my mad steps unafraid
I win no victory in the ranks
Unless you also are repaid

Oh too faithfully following
Sometimes like the most human hound
Or the black vulture whose high wing
Pins my shrinking pride to the ground

I would have been the unearthly angel
Transparent as crystal
Without you: old friend of pain still
Sniffing nothing but evil

I thought one day to launch forth free
From this carcass: but your weight
Puffing black pitch into me
Now the balance reinstates

The more I run the more you chase
Swiftly outstretched in evening glow
Covering all the atlas-face
You urge me still to look at you

And since then you mount you mount
In me taciturn ocean
And with your mortal wave you count
The numbers of my blood's motion

Shadow! From this earth you rise
To nourish me with night not day
With black wine not quenching thirst
And with disgust rotting things away

Alas! I now accept your kiss
Weighting my lids with sleepy breath
Come! Your presence soothes to bliss
Shadow! Loving shadow! Death!

[Translated by JOHN GOULD FLETCHER]

JEAN SANS TERRE
AND HIS SHADOW

(Second Version)

Shadow, brother, shadow,
My companion through all lands
Why don't we, when we stumble,
Hold each other's hands?

I love you as a brother
One womb bore you and me
And I hate you, fleeting, crooked
Grin of perversity

As I run I would kiss you
And I lower my head
But you shrink from me and cower
And I wish that you were dead

Too faithful all-too-human
Dog trotting at my side
Your black-spread vulture's wing
Annihilates my pride

If I could lose you, wretched
Accomplice of my woe
I might be a landless angel
White and pure as snow

Oh to be free of my body
Break loose one day with a bound!
But your weight always tips the balance
I fall back to the pitchy ground

You follow me all the faster
The faster I try to flee you
You cover the globe by evening
And I am forced to see you

I tried to escape in dreams—
Forget you to death
Alas like a soaking sponge
I suck up your damp breath

Since then you rise, you rise
In me like a silent sea
And your wave-beat counts out
My part of mortality

Shadow you rise you touch
My feet, my hands, my knees
Soon you will cover my mouth
Drown me in obscenities

Shadow you rise from the earth
Choose food for my daily lot:
Night, bitter herbs, black salt,
And the black wine of rot

Shadow, angry shadow
Whom all my youth I loved
Why must I sink beneath the wave
Never to rise above?

Alas, I must let you kiss
My eyes with your quieting breath
Already my sleep is peaceful
My loving shadow, my death

[Translated by Robert Wernick]

JEAN SANS TERRE
THE CHEST OF DRAWERS

(First Version)

I am secret-hearted: find me!
Take the keys to the dream-filled drawer
And the safe deposit box of lies
—But who can force the hidden door?

And in this chest, my chest of drawers,
Find albums of forgotten things
And cases of rare eyes, gathered
By one who died for gathering

Here is cotton to smother truth
And wool to weave the fabric hope
And from the tree of liberty
My brother hung himself on this rope

Riddled by tears and like a sieve
My mother's heart is lying here
Beating beside the great gold watch
Of a forgotten ancestor

Here are the tools for every hour:
Saws to sever the hands for hire
And drivers for the screws of faith
And rasps for the screws of desire

A game of cards turned up my queen
The king of spades my luck denied
And I who beat the god at chess
Am done at dice by Ganymede

Another chapel of Saint John
I house tin hearts and hands of wax
And crutches harlots left upon
This altar as they turned their backs

Monsters and heavenless angels
Hide in my heart: their sepulcher
Is locked and I confuse the key
Am I the saint or murderer?

[Translated by GALWAY KINNELL]

JEAN SANS TERRE
THE CHEST OF DRAWERS

(Second Version)

> I am a chest of drawers
> Open to the passerby
> Containing enough to eat and drink
> And above all to die

Here is the bunch of mouldering keys
The bouquet of keys to fields and dreams
Here is the key which locks the door of grace
And the one which will open my tomb again

In this drawer I have the essence of rain
And the spices of the earth
Pepper for killing memories
And shadow—dissolving salt.

In another a gold ancestral watch
The watch time cannot break
Anger Love Nothing stops it
No hammer shatters this dial

Here is the keen edge to sever trust
The wool for mending friendship
But alas I have dropped the stitch
Which could re-weave the wing of innocence

The pack of cards from which my wife emerged
The accountings which prolong the lunar year
And my will written in invisible ink
Will see the notaries of Tartar age

This compass measures the angle of sincerity
And this bell pings for every lie
And here is a life-supply of nails
To crucify the guilty

There I have the bleached heart of my mother
Who always knitted socks for the condemned
And I have the ivory hand of my love
Lost as she leant to wave farewell

The seventh drawer contains the tools of prayer
The gimlet for the worm of temptation
The file against the growth of impoverished thoughts
And the pliers to screw tight the piety of my hands

> I am a chest of drawers
> Locked from the passerby
> Containing enough to doubt and trust
> And above all to die

[Translated by Isabella Gardner]

JEAN SANS TERRE
TO HIS BLACK BROTHER

Brother of night! of milk! my brother!
The earth is blackened by your glance
Your savage cry blackens the air
And women turn black in your love-dance

The Madonna is black and the sunshine
And where you wash the sea is black
And where you drink, black is the wine
And black the sheets beneath your back

Your shadow is pallid at your side
Your black looks blot the sunlight out
And all your days you wear a shroud
Your nakedness your mourning suit

Yet you laugh your great Negro laughter
With the starry whiteness of your grin
And your chaste hands laugh together
As the rhythms of your feet begin

Your laughter erupts like a fountain
Hacks like a saw through steel, forces
Your banks like floods from a mountain
Laughing like magpies and horses

When summer fornicates with the hills
Your blood ferments the wine of sunlight
And the hippo flares your nostrils
And the serpent undulates your feet

In the fields I see you trampling
Black hyacinths, black irises—
Your absolute ruler and king
Tangoing your women to pieces

Stamp your feet! Like echoes of drums
The lava-blooded earth replies:
Soon slaves will win their freedom from
The prisons of their colored bodies

Dance! In fury and tenderness
Kick the same earth that took your tears
And burn in the depths of asphalt eyes
The last of your terrible fears

Spring out of loneliness! Leap
From Harlem, from the universe!
Free yourself! Skin yourself! And strip
Your manhood of its blackened flesh!

Dance out of step! Resist
Perpetual motion, gravity
The march of time! And dance against
The moment's infidelity!

In the night of your flesh you conceal
Thousand-year-old carbons of pain
Now the earth needs your darkness to heal
The pallor of death on its skin

[Translated by GALWAY KINNELL]

JEAN SANS TERRE
GNAWED BY THE VOID

Sleepless I walked the city of asbestos
By the ruined palaces of vast oblivion
That hollow-eyed through its demented windows
Awaited the return of sunken lovers

With steps too old and numb and without weight
I walked in salt that was not even bitter
Widow of recollection that sea-shell
My ear had known the treason of the sea

I was on fire beneath a glacial light
And shook with cold within my sheath of chalk
At the table of Sardanapalus was hungry
And drunken with apostrophes of water

I stumbled on the fallen stone of columns
That formerly held up the roof of time
Among so many others only my spinal column
However seemed to rise from the debris

My shadow that had once been proud and foreign
Clung to me and consoled me there
Like a companion of light conversation
And her invisible eye was on me burning

I followed where her beautiful white hand
With knowing finger pointed towards the north
Was I to love this dream theatrical
The breath of which creates but death?

A grave black crow parched on my vertebrae
Courteous almost with carnivorous beak
Cleansed my thoracic bones of all their shadows
Skillfully as a chisel of white steel

I was familiar now with the inhuman
Solitude of the tree and of the stone
And would have almost blessed the gangrene
That changed my temple and my knees to green

Beneath my coat my being is as void
As any desert overfilled with terror
The dust I was is lost in oxydation
Under the white kiss of the magic-working moon

But at the end of my dull galleries
Day break prepares now to replace the dusk
And brings to life beside my cavities
The rose redeemer of new hope

[Translated by CLARK MILLS]

JEAN SANS TERRE ONE-MAN BAND

I am the One-Man Band
I play with my arms with my legs with my elbows my heels
I play with my fears and my tremblings
You will dance! You will weep!

I am the Man-Accordion
Swollen with joy emptied by sorrow
The cries of all victims are in my lungs
And every death is in my bowels

I am the Man-Organ
Mounting descending again the stairway of the fugue
I am the father of the choir boys
I am the brother of all vespers

I am the Man-Maple
I have a ribbon of birds round my hat
Squirrels in every pocket
The forest forms my escort

I am the Man-River
With my twenty arms I embrace the rivulets
With my twenty legs I enlace the valleys
With my twenty mouths I bite and kiss

I am the Man-Tempest
I throw the lyre-fish into the river
I direct the ballet of waves clicking their castenets
When from her matrix Venus emerges

I am the Man-of-Revolt
In my bagpipes I keep the cries of all the people
My heart in mourning beats the drum
Of the march to liberty

[Translated by Babette Deutsch]

43

JEAN SANS TERRE
BEFORE THE MIRROR

John Landless at the age
Of Christ nailed to the cross
Has no credo or message
His faith at a loss

He's but a poor being
Who eats and who drinks
Without ever knowing
What the world or he thinks

Every day he bathes
In the water of his mirror
But when will it teach him
To see himself clearer?

Oh John of the Earth
Look over your body
A statue of dust
Imbued with energy

A tree whose juice
Rises and falls
And sings without truce
Of your thirty-three springs

From the red roots
To the leaves blond and stark
Your metamorphosis
Consumes the trunk's bark

At the end of your arteries
Flourish the nerves
Your minute capillaries
Seduce cosmic verves

44

Hear the aortas
Ringing the future
And the heart's four doors'
Slow-beating overture

Close the eye-lids
And you will find
Between those borders
A world beyond

The East wind dilates
Your joyful lungs
Scarlet wings which mate
When the knell is rung

Statue of dust
And fountain of blood
Man of Earth's lust
Always growing old

And know the obscure
Law of the vegetable
Which from a creature
Shall turn you to crystal

Under the fontanels
On a low flame
Simmers your tender
God-making brain

But in the orbits
Of your vacant eyes
There dwells the fear
Of Hell's assize

The narrow smile
On your lips feigns
A calmness while
Anger reigns

Your entire carcass
Is filled with the night
When your tired mouth
Rechews sorrow's plight

Although your pupils
Drink of the zenith
Your liver distils
Gall's bitter pith

And while your head
Frustrates the animal
Your trembling skeleton
Founders in evil

Your most sweet pleasure
Your most harsh breath
Your most secret vice
Has the visage of death

Howl for hope
Oh vulnerable worm
When your seed's small scope
Suspends your fleshly term

Your intimate rhythm
Is always transformed
Into unseeing urine
Into milk that has foamed

And suddenly the cycle
Of sovereign creed
Alone makes you holy
The gush of your seed

So then John Landless
Hate and know your wealth
The shadow of substance
Imprisoned in the Self

[*Translated by* ERIC SELLIN]

Drawing by Marc Chagall

JEAN SANS TERRE HAUNTS THE BOULEVARD

Under the chloroform
That numbs delight and fear
The unreal city sleeps
A crumbling Belvedere

Though the tall pantheons
High on the promontory
Shimmer and blaze with neon
Adopt the form of glory

Soon through the labyrinth
Of darkened streets the flood
Of ghosts and shadows rushes
Tinted with rouge and blood

High within the buildings
Alps of glass and stone
The blind who lie in stupor
Dream heavily alone

And closed with bar and shutter
The mountain-dwellers cry
Who walk from door to window
From couch to window: Why

Why do the lemures
Avenging the unknown
In their weak sleep at midnight
Murmur and sigh and moan

And in the silent chambers
As the last lights go out
The ghosts are paired they mingle
Their limbs and frightful doubt

47

Like subterranean waters
Walled by their love from sleep
Alone the red-haired women
Turn in their beds and weep

Elsewhere the men whose pallor
Grows with their remorse
Call for the mother death
And their voice is hoarse

Their foreheads crack and crumble
Like old walls of plaster
Destiny marks early
Those who must meet disaster

The silence that like terror
Lies deeper deeper deeper
Doubles the trance of horror
Of every restless sleeper

When the opaque night
Is streaked with light at last
The candle is blown out
The door yawns that was fast

And the cry that rises
As from deep in earth
Mourns for one life ended
Greets another birth

But so much pain was never
Included in the plan
Under the precipices
Housing the life of man

Wind from the ultimate zone
That filtered through the leaves
Of a nest of willows
Rustles under the eaves

And soft on land and water
And cool near streams and herds
The dawn recalls forever
The timeless voice of birds

[*Translated by* CLARK MILLS]

49

JEAN SANS TERRE ON THE BRIDGE

On the Pont au Change
John Landless turns
His strange face
To the burning water

After the adventure
Of the sevenfold tower
Is he seeking an omen
In the flowing waves?

The waters stride on forever
From the glaciers to the sea
And pass beneath the arches
Of the iron towns

Pass, inexhaustibly
Under the happy bridges
Of the cities of sand
Dancing in a round

John Landless bends down
From night and day
His white face
Over a dark love

What does he see coming down
Tirelessly
Over the fresh fields
Over the oceans?

Nothing but a cadaver
Nothing but a corpse
Seeking a harbour
After too much effort

Trees and briers
Broken furniture
Horns and guts
Of bursted bulls

John Landless leans
His bitter profile
Toward the water pouring
To the great sea

Suddenly his eye
Pierces the current
Which hides and lulls
His burning dream

A pale girl
Smiles under the nets
On her opal skin
The pickerel sleep

Sea weeds and eels
Adorn her hair
And purple fires
Play on her ankles

This heavenly unknown
Who died of fear
Of the lively flight
Of her feeble heart

Her stygian gaze
Calls him and grips him
So that he cries out to her
"Yes! I am coming! I am coming!"

But the passersby go by
Forever over the bridge
And John's tired face
Confounds them all

And one of them comes up
To the divine bum
And slips in his pocket
Two cents for bread

John turns his head
Towards the good man
His heart stormy
His eye haggard and round

But the passersby go by
Over the dense thick river
And their dark mass
Drinks up the individual

John throws himself
Towards the parapet railing
But nothing beats more
In the turgid flux

Oh the sweet miracle
Has ended for ever
Over its tabernacle
Flows a green curtain

On the Pont au Change
John Landless turns
His strange face
To the knowing wind

[Translated by KENNETH REXROTH]

52

JEAN SANS TERRE IN HELL

The anthracite night with
Its black-blooded heart
Denounces the myth
Of our rotting apart

Before the auroras
That will gleam tomorrow
Sleep the Gomorrahs
With death in their marrow

In its bed of pitch
Is nestled the town
With its gods of rich
Bronzes crumbling down

The shadowy crowd
Of the Stygian flow
That clamors aloud
On the banks of Woe

And downflow so compact
Untamable wave
Rush as a cataract
To the subway's cave

Gulp down the mush
Of your meals without sitting
And then quickly rush
To the seasonal rutting

Under the black snow
Bulges out convex
In the bloody fair
An agitated sex

Drawing by Salvador Dali

Listen to the shrug
Of ancient bedsprings
Under the black hug
Of a couple's mergings

There is murdered one Lucifer
For every miscarriage
Avenging a forefather
Thrown to Hell's garbage

Under the padded wad
Of fog's iodine
Decomposes already
A suicide's spine

But the thousand moons
Of underground seas
Do not reveal reasons
For our destinies

From the high walls' width
From earth to eave ooze
Rain and absinthe
And urine and booze

Saltpeter-green shadows
And verdigris tones
Stain the dark windows
Of tenement slums

Incrust yourself: moth
In the zinc, grey
Iron in flesh's bleeding broth
Of the queens of yesterday

Bread becomes pain
Vinegar the wine
Thus the gangrene
Rots all that was fine

City that fattens you
With deep-fried kidneys
The driveling goddess
Of all humanity

I shall be your singer
City I tear apart
I shall be your grave-digger
And roast your heart

I gut you City
And throw your fats
Innards tripes
And spleen to the rats

Here is your Gomorrah
Under rains bloody red
But before the aurora
You John shall have fled

[Translated by Eric Sellin]

JEAN SANS TERRE
MEETS AHASUERUS

One day John Landless meets with
That ancient under the curse
Ahasuerus brother
Of this old universe

Ahasuerus strolling
Daily in festive tog
Parades his trailing greatcoat
To the ghetto synagogue

At home in New York or Cairo
Wherever he may stray
He is the sole possessor
Of every passing day

That God exists is certain
Who blessed him after His whim
And if God is not surely
Man has elected Him

For if the matter is doubtful
It is better by far to pray
A prayer is less costly
Than pity anyway

The old man loves this earth
And all he is bound to do
The bitter herbs of repentance
Are not too tough to chew

With vinegar or with honey
He loves his dish of carp
He loves the sounding strings
Of rude Ezekiel's harp

He loves the old rituals
As he loves liberty
He loves to hasten onward
Clothed in solemnity

Hatred he loves and the venom
Of whose sure power he dreamt
He loves whatever gives rein to
His most supreme contempt

In each of the world's ghettoes
He has his royal seat
But he must live by begging
With vast words for his meat

From the Amazon returning
To his own street unbidden
He is greeted by all the neighbors
Not one keeps a secret hidden

He has the prophet's wisdom
Who knows what love must be
But everywhere and always
He interprets it differently

His people are common people
He watches to see spring
From the shame and blame they suffer
A youth who moves like a king

The son of a diamond-cutter
He will cut with his diamond eye
Even the hardest stones
And the pride of those who are high

To avenge his fathers forever
Penned in a filthy sink
This revolutionary
Will take blood for his drink

His too plump sister waiting
Behind the lowly door
Feels her heart's wisdom ripen
Gently more and more

Ruth lives on and Rachel
Lives in this pure profile
That speaks of the living waters
From the Jordan to the Nile

For still that virtue prospers
Fed by her generous breast
The strength of the mighty mothers
Of the people whom God blest

Under the opaque heaven
The accursed ghetto bears
On the sixth thousandth Easter
You renew that splendour of theirs

All are sisters and brothers
To be reborn no fear
With the reviving primrose
Every spring of the year

A whole people utters
An anguished garlicky cry
For deliverance calling
Upon ADONAI

New pious Ahasuerus
After many a fast will nod
To young John Landless bidding
Him taste the wine of God

He brays the savory spices
The lamb without spot he slays
The sacrifice he rejoices
To make for the holy days

This is the bread of affliction
The egg means hope to endure
Everything moves to music
Song that bleeds and is pure

But with the dawning morrow
This man of a thousand years
Once more will bear to Gomorrah
A grief too heavy for tears

Thus John Landless meeting
Ahasuerus the Jew
Recognized perhaps his brother
But flesh of his flesh he knew

[Translated by BABETTE DEUTSCH]

JEAN SANS TERRE
CALLS FOR THE CYCLOPS

Become a Cyclops once more
Smooth-templed brother
Build up Europe from the floor
Old dreams wither

Look! your mother the Earth
Has meager breasts
But for giving you birth
Let her name be blessed

Black down to the roots
The stark raving trees
Drink benzine and booze
Disguised as a breeze

Lysol streams
And oxide clouds
Choke earth's dreams
Under death's grave shroud

Putrescent breath
And foul blood reveal
The sickness unto death
Of the age of steel

The wretchedness of life
And the acrid sweat that grinds
Away the workers' courage
In the saltpeter mines

Listen to the plaints
Of hospital suffering
Hoping like saints
For the votive offering

61

Adorable madonnas
Like a cross on their beds
Are nursing their ulcers
Near lily-pure breasts

Silently syphilis
Down the hall leaps
With an iodine kiss
The whole ward sleeps

In the city metallic
With great tunnels sown
The hydrocephalic
Braves the unknown

Rivers of come
Shot without lust
The girders be-scum
And the walls incrust

Night's lover copulates
With ardent spouse
Death patiently waits
In the hair of a louse

Oh pray that shall rise
The vitalizing sap
Before everything dies
Smothered by crap

Let miracles come
And ecstatic yellings
Searchlights whose beam
Clears ghost-ridden dwellings

Spill golden oils
All over the city
And halo-like coils
Of electricity

One hundred thousand tons
Of heart and concrete
Built the towering columns
That clutter the street

From the ruins of plaster
Up out of the night
From the shadows a master
Man will surge bright

Behold the man! Admire
His eye undefiled
A smile blossoms like fire
From his lips of a child

His step which resounds
In May's happy park
His hand which abounds
With friendship's spark

Delivered from doubt
The people long ignored
Will walk on the route
With spirit restored

And under the splendour
Of the sky newly starred
You may follow the funeral
Of a century abhorred

[*Translated by* ROBERT NURENBERG]

JEAN SANS TERRE
MANUFACTURER OF NIGHT

And range on smoky range
Of solid dark has night
Salts pits hollows beds
Of mythy anthracite

This towering abyss
That up to heaven fell
Continues above blue
The red mines under hell

Hides a lyric and
Strong gold malleable
To long hammering
By man miserable

But if the dark has mines
Industry has man
He can grind the evening's
Shattered loss of sun

His manufactures shine
With inutility
Night gifts souvenirs
For nonentity

Wheels of fever whirl
By some kindness moved
Pulverize the dream
Of the last beloved

For to get an ounce
Of love's pale delight
You must smelt a thousand
Tons of nitric night

Into the casting furnace
Into night's afternoon
One must pitch distracted
Odd ends of the moon

Then break into the orange
Basements of Algol
Steel for fiercer smelting
The new alcohol

When a meteor
Splits the firmament
Meadows of phosphorus
Burn a new incense

But the black snow falls
Our hearts collapse
We must drink the scented
Fatal drops

In the coal crevasses
Parthenons impious
Old and thundered crags
Swag of Prometheus

Tapping the urine
Of mammoths from
Drunken pipelines
Gushes petroleum

Sweeping the whole structure
Massive brick on brick
Night and sweating city
Pittsburgh of Old Nick

From the highest
Of old Uranus' hills
The crime-bearing tempests
Lash our bare skulls

Thus John Landless
Has tried
Exploiting nights of loneliness
Satanic pride

[*Translated by* Lionel Abel]

JOHN DEATH

I run to the plains
That are loud with streams
Where fountains climbing
Tell their dreams

I enter the dark
And quiet glade
Of the tribes of the dead
The peoples of shade

There under the ivy
The bare veined stone
My youthful father
Keeps watch alone

Beneath the delirium
Of glow-worms' light
His patient smile
Braves endless night

The whole universe
In him resounds
Autumnal voices
And winter sounds

By a howling storm
Are the heavens torn?
Or is it the blare
Of Gabriel's horn?

Of a sudden the brown
Night deepens to gray
The full moon reddens
And rots away

Drawing by Salvador Dali

Biblical tomb
Will you open for me
To the probing bomb
Of memory?

Beneath a black star's
Total eclipse
Do I hear a descending
Apocalypse?

The alders dance
Distinct and clear
Already their trance
Awakens my fear

Church steeples nearby
With heads of tin
Nod bunches of bells
Like mannikins

Sorcerer owls
Their eyes open wide
From the willows watch
On every side

"Father!" I cry
In my mad monotone
While an owl coughs
On its perch of stone

Then among brambles
John Dying John Death
My feeble body
Sinks to the earth

[Translated by WILLIAM JAY SMITH]

JEAN SANS TERRE
DISCOVERS THE ANGEL

Son of a nebula
And the great Altair
The Earth is hollow
And fills me with fear

The sky's cow bellows
Expelling the hills
And throws me back down
To the pit where slime spills

My star was planted
Between slim thighs
And in the precipice
That all men comprise

I know from which cave
I issued to light
My bones quake and rave
Under their tunic of spite

Painfully armed
With a soul and with vertebrae
I have been justly banished
By the warmth of the tenebrae

And my foot feels out
On the continent's top
The route that hastens
Toward life's final stop

Everywhere I see my brothers
Linger lightly on the ridge
Of dust and earth
Which they cannot abridge

Clinging to their dust
Which shields them with its might
They avoid without lust
The dangers of the light

As for me, I stagger
Fearing I'll defile
The shadow of the swallow
Which touched me for a while

The valiant lark
Lands on my head
And from my eyes
Pecks the fire's red

The knowing nuggets
Of ship-wrecked stars
Which in the night
Reveal my scars

And my ancestor-trees
Elephant-limbed sires
Soothe my old age
With its childish desires

Throw me down oranges
And small satellites
Food for the angels
In these depths far from lights

Groping in the cosmos
With my leprous hand
I wrong the last hour
Throw my bones in the sand

Out towards the blueness
Of archangels guerdoned
I return home blessed
Pardoned and unburdened

[Translated by Eric Sellin]

71

JEAN SANS TERRE
WRAPS HIMSELF IN A RED COAT

Coming toward you in my red coat
Do not ask me if I wear the mantle of the king of Tyre
Or the cloak of the beggar of Benares
My coat is lined with love

The song of love goes before me as crimson dust
Precedes the sirocco which trails the sulphurous storm
It breathes above the seven couching hills
Before astounding the valleys of thirst dried up by Satan

For it is a wind of anger that swells my bloody coat
And flares my pine torch from the forest's depths
I carry vengeance to the people who still dream
In the strangled slums, in the hangars of nightmare

In the flophouses of the Beggar's Court
In the bazaars where hang the carpets blood-stained
By the thousand-year-old hand of slaves
In the prisons cemented by tears and petrified skulls

I light I light with my dancing torch
The tarnished skies of the cities
For the poor who exist on the thirst of others
And have not the right to be thirsty

Those who peddle the song of apples
Of milk of rain of air and the coca of the Trusts
Those who sell exactly enough to die,
To dress the abscessed wounds of their children

I come I come on my red horse
Whose wings are put together with flaps
Torn in strips from my heart, from my vagabond's coat . . .
His hoofs flower the rock to a rosebush of love

His nostrils breathe fire from the stars to you
I come from the depths of the forever virgin forest
And I kindle for you all the birds of my crown
The fire of the lyre-bird and the golden fire of the phoenix

A universal Saint Elmo's fire
To spark men's dust
To portion joy to all the corners of the world
To wrap you, my brothers, in a crimson coat

[*Translated by* ISABELLA GARDNER]

JEAN SANS TERRE
CITIZEN OF DREAMS

Although John Landless
I'm not spared the lease
Of earthly laws:
Food and decease

Mournful mammal
Swollen with lust
Whose flesh wants only
To turn to dust

Life is but a fight
Against the flowing sweat
And the horrible might
Of gravity's threat

How then, Dionysos, do you sate
Your body heavy as stones
Sluggish with the weight
Of two hundred and twenty-two bones?

All this avid flesh that
Gnaws at time without forgetting
The pulling taut
Of the wrinkles' netting?

Am I but a man
To stand beside bins
Weighing market apples
Instead of sins?

If sometimes I try
To punish evils
Within my belly
An animal squeals

But wherever I carry
This burdened heart
A cohort of shadows
Tears it apart

Then under these rags
That cover my slime
Is suddenly heard
My best demon's rhyme

Out of my bitter blood
That sours on the floor
Fleeing the prison mud
My gliding spirits soar

Quietly my head
Lawless in the firmament
Turns among the planets
Joining in the tournament

Rising towards the moon
And frozen stratospheres
Like a fire-balloon
I transcend my fears

It's I who've betrayed
And forsaken my thoughts
My soul makes a trade
With the heavenly vaults

Muscles and basalts
No longer have meaning
When the soul exalts
Beyond God's pleading

Farther than doubt
Farther than faith
Abducting my route
And myself like a wraith

Oh I walk ahead
With a resolute foot
Among the systems
Of a pure absolute

A citizen of dreams
In its palaces of blue
I abjure the life-stream
That troubled me so

I make myself lawless
As I become John
Utterly landless
Angel within

[*Translated by* ERIC SELLIN]

JEAN SANS TERRE ON THE PEAKS

Since Landless John
Never snatched of the broad
Acres upon
Earth, one square rod

He is seeking those crests
Whence, numbed, to the high
Gods man casts
The insult of his cry

Whistle of the young blast
Through his heart blows
His the most
Exquisite blossom of snows

The larch dropped its shade
Slender, high
On its hillock-top, that weighed
Less there than colours of sky

And printed in small
Ice-circlets one reads, almost
With tears, here the frail
Chamois have passed

He has mastered it at last
The summit, Landless John!
Before him abased
Earth's hugeness sweeps down

A hundred peaks ring round
Him their dance
Till his forehead is crowned
With a scintillance

Shall he king it for one
Hour, then of a day?
O he's heartsick too soon
It's too foolish a sway

Already it dismays
The vista of such
Unanimous splendours. The space
Golds, grandeurs, all too much

This peak so absolute
Earlier in seduction
Melts under his boot:
The defection of stone

The potent glacier leaks
A sordid stream
The plains of steel go bleak
With the dying out of flame

Among those Wests it is,
Beneath, there form to view
The envisioned countries
Canaans that are true

Lights go on there and shine
In the heights that are sovereign ones
Down there the jewels they mine
Are genuine stones

Down there, Landless John
The crowd is, that wants
You, where man earths in
Remote from the elements

A mist slides over
Its rosying hazes
Softly it covers
A continent with roses

How hard it is
To be great, and to be one!
Down there a thousand cities
Call you back to them: John!

Quick, the descent!
Time to be gone
Bursting to repent
In the night of ashes to cower down

Beneath, Landless John
Beneath, not here
Joys are full-grown
Where you are not, there!

[Translated by Léonie Adams]

JEAN SANS TERRE
AT THE EDGE OF THE ROAD

The path of my disquiet
Wanders the open plain
The end of kilometers
Is not the end of pain

Where so much fallen wreckage
Litters an earth too old
I seek beneath a streetlamp
My shadow in the cold

Past the meridian
Past the unending marches
My hapless solitude
Trembles under the arches

My white-faced solitude
Faithful in spite of all
Whose clipped wings lie folded
Under a worn shawl

[Translated by CLARK MILLS]

JEAN SANS TERRE
IN THE PRESENCE OF
SPRING AND DEATH

John Landless leave
Your longing and alarms
Hold the four seasons close
In your two arms

For when the daybreak
Stirs and flowers and burns
And tinged with gold and fire
Life returns

Then from the crowded dead
The living throng
Doubt is mistaken
And the night is wrong

Amidst the dry grass
On the narrow slope
The green stalk of the crocus
Leaps like hope

The pious mayflower
That all things amaze
Stares outward from the meadow
Sleeps and prays

The lily in the valley
Rings the bell
Deep in the rock
The crystal organs swell

And the grave alder-trees
In congregation
Repeat the psalm
Of the new dispensation

As for a wedding
The green fields unfold
Strike in the dandelion
Medals of gold

And the most wretched willows
Bent and bowed
Feel birds upon their shoulders
And are proud

O my friend whose destruction
Grows within
Charged with albumin
Eaten by chagrin

Whose limbs are stiffening
Whose hair falls out
Who sense your death inside
Immense as doubt

Who hear the enamel
Crumble from your tooth
And who are saved
By no semblance of truth

Who in the melted marrow
Of your bones
Know that your life lies low
As fallen stones

Is this your voice
That sings along the way
Where pass the communicants
At break of day

Who kneel where the white clover
Shines like mirth
And press the exhausted skull
On the moist earth

O let your heavy head
Fall to the grass
Where amidst violets
The huge bees pass

For you resemble
Flowers in the afternoon
Convict or saint
The dark is coming soon

Know that your spirit
Will find life again
In the mimosa
In the stag's voice near the glen

From the blue seedlings
Of your planted eyes
The myosotis
Mirrors the blue skies

The trembling columbine
That grows apart
Borrows a deeper shadow
From your heart

And when at last you lie
Under the mound
Deep in oblivion
Oh drenched and drowned

Poor John you will forget
The loud alarms
And that the earth fled from you
In her arms

[Translated by CLARK MILLS]

JEAN SANS TERRE
CURSES AUTUMN

How many autumns have comprised
Your death with such force
That you are no longer surprised
By any remorse

That so many feasts
Don't prevent you from knowing
The skeletal breast
And the ultimate tolling

For exuberance excites
The hand of destiny
And all of your flights
Fall into Vengeance Sea

Already the centaurs
Stamping their hoofs
Make chlorine gush
From the tombs' ancient roofs

Proffering to storms
Their stalwart poitrel
Their laughter worms
The evening coral

But ecstasy is brief
The glutted heart pulses
With an increasing grief
And the boiling of pus

An awful presage
Embraces the forest
Its beggarly rage
Returns without rest

In putrefaction
And in blindness
All creation
Finds its truthfulness

An infamous cream
Satan's spit
Spreads with a gleam
On the pale earth's grit

All the twilight
Drinks up a flood
Of abscessed mushrooms
Overlaid with blood

The frightful Boletus
And Orange-agaric
Of felts and sponges
Distill their milk

Once a ballerina
Rustling like dancers
The chaste dog-rose
Is covered with cankers

And like the universe
The apples' round forms
Submit to the ravenous
Hunger of worms

Majestic oak trees
Become gibbets which are hung
With queens and sentries
And ballads we've sung

With a flap of its feathers
The cruel wind flies
And smashes our ladders
That tempted the skies

In the high-banked vineyards
Baked by Hell's sight
Has settled down
The beast of the night

All the gold of dawns
Reduced to ingots
Evaporates and is gone
In the fire of fagots

And the gnarled rain
Betrayed by the summer
Doesn't speak of it again
But shall always remember

Drunk with vengeance
Without a misgiving
It buries with incense
The brood of the living

And the leaves wan and tired
Of trembling at the breeze
That plucks them with desire
Are ravished with ease

In their fall slow like breath
In the late autumn sky
The kindness of death
Gives them power to fly

[Translated by Eric Sellin]

JEAN SANS TERRE UNMASKS SLEEP

Funerally wreathed, the naked serpent
Has settled down already in my sleep
That seems his estuary and repose
And watches flowing every daybreak leap

Deep in my breast he coils his writhing nest
Fraternally almost to calm pretends
I sleep divinely sleep and fail to guess
The hour when self's own semblance ends

A glutton is it swells upon my substance
And dreams have only fallen into line
To make me drowsy numb my watchful sense
And let the demon mark me with his sign?

But far from me like that balloon ascending
My head drifts from my body well apart
And rises light and very frail
And still my gaze lives on within the heart

Sometimes I see me swarming all in vermin
Sometimes escape I pure into beyond
But who then inexorably compels me
To heed the angel holds me to my bond?

Am I that flesh or lava poured from crater
Or merely the one resonance of name?
Am I a larva or enduring plasm
Voracious depths that swallow all the same?

I sleep: from heel to head quicksilver runs
In purple through the night where I belong
My quickened pulse the formula reveals
Of what my lyre shall pick as its last song

It's better to be blind to his disgrace
Ignore the term for honouring what's signed
At the adventure's end the bill that's drawn
On absolute is paid in paper fine

Far wiser from the shadows to withhold
Our saddened sense of life's oblivion
The words that froth upon lips
Like foam illumining the wrinkled ocean

Pure gold alone, the gold of fireflies in
The night that trace the truth or change to smoke
Wherein all unions soon are new remade
And the insane at last are stripped of cloak

Rein back the four mares turned the chariot
Beneath their saturnalian hooves that crash
All fused now in the prodigy's new spark
And all the daily papers crumbling ash

One love, one love alone Prometheus
Sufficed to save us from that horrid empire
From all-of-matches-forest struck ablaze
Leapt the inhuman mystery of fire

[Translated by GEORGE REAVEY]

JEAN SANS TERRE
REVIEWS THE FATHERS

Our fathers liked to carry persian beards
Between the beards old cigars and old words
They liked the chicken soup and marrow bone
And then to stay at God's diamond throne

They sold green herring and they bought black suits
But God was ever present in disputes
The hurricane was hidden over the land
When any sin grew in their skin or gland

They were the fathers but they were the fool
To worship glassware or a rag of wool
They used the oaks to hang a man with thoughts
They used the river to look at the clouds

What worth is life but to account odd coins
To dig the earth to burn her oils
To fabricate thin web for tears of girls
To carve one's nails to curb one's curls

Their daughters wore silk over unknown sores
And healed behind the throat the song of whores
Their sons despised the herrings and the gods
Lost battles of the future in their cods

Meanwhile the fathers curled their flowering beards
Sold coal and slag bought orchards oaks and birds
Built palaces drank wine ate steak
And didn't sin—but earth began to quake

One day the tyrant came—the hurricane
The fathers' beards were strewn o'er street and lane
Their door stayed open like a mouth of drowned
Only the dogs remained and mourned around

Well thousand fathers
Their daughters and their sons are gone are gone
Their savior himself vanished at the wall
But swallows came back after all

[*Translated by* WILLIAM CARLOS WILLIAMS]

JEAN SANS TERRE'S
HYMN TO THE SUN

The shadows of death
Lay over my sleeping
When your ecstasy—
Golden—hit my waking

When your eye struck
The walls of the shrine
Eye of which I know
The third and final sign

Egg of Genesis
Rise from the rich earth
Let your densest yellow
Hatch your shell's girth

And fall like a bomb
With its charge of magic
Into the catacomb
Where I lie lethargic

Ring, oh kettle-drum
Against my tympanum
Change me to Dedalus
Send me where he is from

Pour out radium
In my blackest tares
And with your helium
Quick cure my scars

I now feel your amber
The oil of your love
Soften my members
Dull my hell's blood

All this is sacred food
A dizzying cup
The bay by the fountain
Calm fruit which we sup

Let me devour them
Let me then eat these
Meteor currants
And planet-like cherries

For my own libation
The pomegranate grows
The apple the melon
And the muscadel rows

Ten thousand sunrays
Have rendered them ready
To render me better
With wines sweet and heady

You give me your substance
You open me in turn
To your vast abundance
Great star where Love's born!

[Translated by ERIC SELLIN]

JEAN SANS TERRE
SACRIFICES HIMSELF TO THE SUN

John Landless adores
The adolescent star
The drunken twilight
Of rising centuries

It is the terrible eye
The single eye in the forehead
Of the unnameable being
That we know nothing about

It is the egg of Genesis
The egg of all eggs
The kiss of wood-embers
The wedding-party of fire

It is the dynamite
Which in cities
Replaces the myth
With the truth

It is the mad bomb
Whose explosion
Overturns the tombs
Redeeming them

And although without a country
For his thin body
John covers the earth
As the dead do

Conqueror of dawns!
He cries: Great Sovereign!
Descend and devour
My sterile grain

Always I eat thee
In the black currant
In the sweet orange
Without giving thanks

In the bitter pomegranate
By thee made pregnant
And in the muscade grape
I drink thee forever

And in the gooseberry
And in the melon
Everywhere thou sleepest
In these little suns

But because I love thee
In my poor hunger
Punish this blasphemy
Revenge thyself at last

Drink from eyelids
Enchanted honey
The great light
Of the human will

Dry and compress
Ancestor of Minos
My muscle and fat
Down to rock and bone

Gnaw with thy beasts
Ants and vultures
My skeleton entire
My pride and love

Twist grind and tan
My livid flesh
Which already withers
In its golden rags

So that from me will flow
Blood and pus
To nourish and make drunk
The replete angels

Descend and flay me
Grand inquisitor
Make me the torch
Of mortal happiness

If thou freest me
From wicked blood
My flesh which is dear to me
Consents to perish

I do not wish to rot
As a satrap any longer
After the banquets
I know how to die

Set on fire and burn
In the divine fire
Of thy owl-light
All that was so vain

Sun I invite thee
And I submit
Bring me back to life
Never never more

[Translated by LOUISE BOGAN]

JEAN SANS TERRE
WEDS THE MOON

(First Version)

Often late at night
John Landless drinks
The beer of moonlight
That foams in silence

He drinks it drop by drop
He drinks it straight and strong
But he drinks from the cup
Of doubt and anguish long

For the solitary man's fate
Is eternal thirst
Nothing can satiate
The drinker of love

The far-spread liquid
The colour of cream
Denies empty hearts
Its runaway dream

And too much light
Only puts a veil
On the thousand-fold secret
Of the starry angel

Inoxydizable moon
Oh helium rose
Your snow from the sand of dunes
Spins us a peplos

The spirit of the seas
Is reabsorbed in you
Your metamorphoses
Dictate our law

An amazon's breast
White and virginal
For which man's zest
Invents new evil

Heavy with a love bitter
From Belphagor's force
Your panther has a litter
Of dogs of remorse

You nurse the race
Which we must fear
The voracious breed
Of a dark Nadir

The young planets
Of the boreal nest
Suckle smiling
At your sparkling breast

But on tired nights
When you thin by the hour
Your pitcher breaks
And your milk turns sour

Woman making women weak
Submissive to your blood
On these nights your soul
Offers itself to the meek

The voice of the barn owls
Torments your fearing dreams
And in the osier beds
The shadow of steams

Under the meteor's wake
Extinguished by night-time
Become a mandrake
In a bed of thyme

Moon forever red
Mortal by seasons
You spatter our heads
With pale poisons

So thus John Landless
The insatiate madman
Becomes John Lunar
And your sad husband

[Translated by ERIC SELLIN]

JEAN SANS TERRE
WEDS THE MOON

(Second Version)

Often Landless John
Drinks at night
The lunar beer
That foams light

Drinks drop by drop
The narcotic brew
Doubt also drinks
And anguish too

For the solitary
Shall always thirst
Yet never quenched
Who drinks love first

The pale liquor
Fills everywhere
Empty hearts
With a lost dream's flare

But too much splendour
Only veils
The thousand mysteries
Of starry angels

Stainless moon
Lotus of ether
Your snow of sand
Burns our flesh

Your amazon breast
Smooth, virginal
Makes men
Lovers of evil

With lewd love swelled
By Belphegor
Dogs of remorse
Your panther bore

You nourish the Nadir's
Sombre, rude,
Vicious, man-
Destroying brood

But the nights when your face
Grows drawn and thin
Your pitcher breaks
Your milk turns green

The lovers' fervors
Disappear
All your magic
Turns to fear

You are no more
The fatal redhead
Your beer spumes
With venom tainted

Your golden palaces
Crumble down
The world of the shadows
Dies into dawn

[Translated by YVAN AND CLAIRE GOLL]

JOHN THE HERMAPHRODITE

John the two-faced
John of double meaning
Knows not by whom he's embraced
Nor towards what fate he's leaning

For he cracks the endless night
Beyond the orbit of himself
A frail hermaphrodite
He breaks all laws like fragile delft

Does he know if he is double
Or only half in fact?
And when disturbed by trouble
If all goes through the act?

Never a unit tamed
And never authentic
As soon as he's claimed
He makes his escape

In solitude two-fold
Since the time of division
He must forever withhold
The impossible confession

The ardor to seduce
The fate to be abducted
Both he can reproduce:
He is Romeo and Juliet

Pretence for a male
His virility is shed
At the touch of a pale
Hand preparing the bed

He is one and the other
The river's swift flowing
The banks that smother
The flesh of the morning

The sun of another land
Fattened and green
Slumbers near at hand
Making him keen

When everything is desexed
And so nothing can hide
The opposite has annexed
Its complementary side

John who was the faun
Becomes the nymph too
A yellow-laughing Pan
Where the myosotis grew

Does this Narcissus who eyes
His image in the water
Know that in his thighs
An anguish grows hotter?

When an artful odor comes
From under his arms
His brother-hand succumbs
To its sister's charms

Impalpable gesture
Whose silent singing
Consumes the incest
Of the transformed being

[Translated by Eric Sellin]

JEAN SANS TERRE FILLS HIS BELLY

But as things go
Since one must eat
In the lower intestine
Your vengeance can flow

Delectable eating
Will chase away death
Which roams about whipping
In your body's depth

Your jaw severs
The strength of an ox
Your tongue shivers
At eggs' golden rocks

With your handsome teeth
Bite the tender quail
Young partridge speckled bright
Which you ardently assail

Scrape the rabble's garlic
Unbind the bulbs in store
That every season's sowing
Might show its basic core

The shallot sheds its skin
And the gentle dill seed
On the barbecued pig
Will whet your greed

Gulp down silks
And pale white velvets
Curdled milks
And butter pellets

Run to the wedding
To gobble the lobster
And then to the warmth
Of the funeral parlor

And under the carillons
Of feasts loud and hale
Feel how the morning fruit
Suddenly grows frail

Yes with tripe
And wine on your breath
Wage your battle
Against feeble death

[Translated by ERIC SELLIN]

LANDLESS AND WIFELESS
DON JUAN

Don Juan Landless
Loves a thousand and three
And nevertheless
How alone is he

Does he love the virgin
With the eyes like a squirrel's?
Does he love the widow
Flushing under mourning veils?

Does he love the silk
Of an avid flesh?
The black tulip?
Or Hell's pulpy mesh?

Does he want the pomegranate
With thirty-six hearts?
The pale Naiad whose sisters
Are thirty-six bards?

Diana of the Louvre
Mistress of the wind?
She whom a glove's touch
Can easily bend?

The broker's fat wife
On the balcony?
Or the baker's bride
Freckled full of glee?

Here is Gabrielle
Svelte with her charm
Lodging the summer spell
Under her arm

Does he want the amethyst
Of an iridescent hand?
Or the saddening fist
Of a bronze turned to sand?

Here are the anemones
Smelling of incenses
And here is the nun who flees
Her five burning senses

Is it a slanting eye
Which drives him mad?
Or the street girl
Who can always be had?

Don Juan: you worship
What you haven't got
But flesh you touched yesterday
Will rot and decay

Burn up your legend
Of invincible passion
Absence is greater and
Victorious in its fashion

Oh to make you drunk
Don Juan the beau
Release and debunk
Ennui's eternal flow

Furious infidel
Resist its charms
Absence has wings
You have but arms

Flee the slim prison
Of so many thighs
Flee: take revenge on
Your swooning and sighs

Even Cleopatra
With the serpent's cameo
Will make you a hearth
Of her gay seraglio

But Pegasus whinnies
In the meadows of flight
Towards other ecstasies
In the patch-work of the night

Caress the shoulders
Of virginal crests
And seduce the glacial boulders
Of polar breasts

Defy the tempest
And the wind that's virile
And engulf your head
In the naked of the Nile

Landless Don Juan
Wifeless with nothing
Who venerates nothing
Venereal Man

[Translated by ERIC SELLIN]

BALLAD OF JOHN THE EXILED

I am John without a country
To the old tribe born
Who wanders without baggage
In a void without bourne

How many ancestors
Walked lived died
On the road I follow
As the dice shall decide

They rise from death's shadow
From caves out of time
Of Erebus relating
A riddle of slime

And of the patriarchs
The pious godson
I plod on and on
Peremptorily alone

Neither slow Jordan
Nor Ganges in spate
Can change or deflect
The course of fate

From summit to sepulcher
From tract to tall town
This haughty loneliness
Will never down

I hold a bare staff
In a sweating hand
How narrow is earth
How naked the land

Frontiers are closing
Through the world entire
And the harried confront
Brakes of barbed wire

Neither the just mount
Nor Sharon's dreaming air
Go with the pariah
As he flees otherwhere

Neither the green Danube
Nor Mississippi's mud
Can disperse my distaste
With all their flood

To pick up wormwood
I left the trail
I composed fifths
For the nightingale

In kitchens I've seen
Copper gleam reflect
In the quilted recesses
Beds in muslin decked

I slept under yew
I prayed under palm
Nowhere shall my heart
Retrieve its calm

[Translated by JOHN PEALE BISHOP]

JEAN SANS TERRE
CONFRONTED BY LOVE

Woman be my mother
Woman be my sea
Sea in which I suffer
Loss in which hope lives for me

Sea to which flow rivers
Tired of conquering the sky
Sea where finally go rivers
To slowly, chastely die

After so much wandering
To be cast in with you
After all the suffering
And the disarrays too

Open the delta locks
And let the water through
Oh woman don't resist
Him who once extolled you

Knowing accomplice
To my masochist's eye
Glorify vice
With a lingering sigh

If you bare your body
Down to your mind
Suddenly solitude
Is left behind

Our sweet Lady
Who guesses all
Never condemned
Our innermost gall

Lie under my downpour
Bog of which I'm prey
And be a shelter for
The tired beast at bay

Now the anemone
Which my feet crush on the ground
Now the amazon
Whose glance strikes me down

You who were the pure pole
Of a clarity unframed
My nail caresses you
And your body is tamed

Under your armpit
May the unique liqueur
Which flows near your heart
Reserve me its fervor

In wheat which bows
Beneath the windy spear
May your sadness know
That I am near

In the blood of the berry
Sweet on your palate
Your lips caress me
To their heart's content

And when the owl
Looses its sad howl
It's I who am sent
To make you lament

So if I give you up
To the hands of the night
My pale druidess
It's there I alight

There beneath your door
My shadow waits, bent
On the evening which
Brings your consent

Woman be my mother
Oh woman be my sea
In which John Fatherless
Ceases to be

[*Translated by* ERIC SELLIN]

JOHN WITH NO MOON

By the light of the moon
John who has no other
Meanders from one
City to another

Alone forever
Drunk with infinity
He wanders the world over
In exile eternally

Form linked with form
In pairs all except him
Sleep under the chloroform
Of a senseless dream

The moonlight shows
Courts and corridors
Golden windows
And platinum doors

Over the rooftiles
In the heart's core
The star spills
The oil of extreme languor

Oh even
The prison grills
Glow with crime
Like live coals

Only John keeps walking walking
With a mist wrapped around him
And finds nothing
But a bridge to shelter him

Always while he was young
His ambition was too great:
To grow drunk with tasting
Some pure absolute

Always vague, some height
Or arcane in his head
He even forgot
To make a bed

The sky all hung with lights
Turns like a fool
The radiant planets
Reveal jewel upon jewel

But John does not pause
To watch the cosmic lake
Head down he goes
His tired feet ache

Old all of a sudden
Chewing his spite
Poor John with no moon
Founders in the night

[Translated by W. S. Merwin]

JEAN SANS TERRE
THE PRODIGAL SON

(First Version)

Now John quits the Tantalid city
With an empty bag but a heavy heart
The fountain's evil eye is devoid of pity
The customs men search golden eyes that smart

In the kitchen he left his woebegone mother
His darling drowning in the mirror alone
Forever the garden his nasturtiums will smother
And the dream hangs itself in the closet at dawn

Whom is he seeking? The blacksmith of morn?
The glazier to patch up the years as they die?
The farrier of the plesiosaurus bygone?
The clock-smith who makes time putrefy?

He swallowed the white bread before the black
His left hand refuses to wash the right
He ate the eggs of the phoenix and the tail of the jack
At the foot of the gallows grows his flower blue and white

He gets off at the hotel his head white-tressed
He meets mystery's queen: a pearl
Whom he kills without having once possessed
In his flight he leaves his past with the hat-check girl

One evening at the bar he remembers the hawthorne
Which only burned for him in one garden awhile
He takes the express: enters the kitchen at dawn
His dead mother receives him with a heavenly smile

[Translated by ROBERT NURENBERG]

115

JEAN SANS TERRE
THE PRODIGAL SON

(Second Version)

John leaves the city of the Tantalids
Where the sacred ox hangs on walls of fire
Beds grieve in the depths of empty palaces
And man dies of thirst beside an enchanting river

John leaves his family with their elbows on the table
Blaspheming the gods while eating their birds
He betrays his mother's lovely smile
And leaves his mistress drowned in her mirror

What does he seek? The delirious cities
The forests of desire? The birth-giving harbors?
The desert sands? The dreadful tempest?
The ill fortune which in turn is seeking him?

He wished to measure the thickness of silence
The weight of thought the colour of grief
To root up the tree of knowledge
To falsify dice of fate to reverse the law of brass

All the trades: to knead the bread of patience
To dampen the wine of great enchantment
To solder the handle of friendship to embroider destiny
To embrace all things without becoming their lover

He wished to ravish everything to fill soul and belly
To drink the sea and swallow fire
To be the singing bird and the thinking reed
To know a heaven without acknowledging God

But one evening at an inn, his hair having turned white
He met himself alone in a frozen mirror
Surrounded by his fears his omissions his unpaid bills
He died in giving back all he had snatched away

[*Translated by* LOUISE BOGAN]

JEAN SANS TERRE
THE PRODIGAL SON

(Third Version)

John quits his city by the Port of Doubt
Quits by Oblivion's port his continent
He has thrown his shadow to the roadside ants
And given his dead to the flames and does not repent

He flees the tower clocks whose hands have vanished
The furnaces that are smelters of the dawn
The tinsmiths tinkering at the chimera
The gardens of love whence all the girls are gone

He's devoured his white bread before the black was eaten
Of the carp's head and the pike's tail had his fill
He has tasted the salt of the earth and the pepper also
But the spirit of earth remains a secret still

He has gulped the eagle's egg and fried the egg of fable
The egg of Columbus he broke the Phoenix egg he cracked
Yet his flesh was ever avid and vulnerable
Though on the Stygian stream his wake was tracked

At the shady "Hotel Cytherea" he finally lands
He straps his empty valise in the morning carefully
And carrying only sobs and wrongs and wrinkles
Embraces the woman and mocks her mystery

Then he leaves he runs he tumbles he sinks turning
Toward sunset toward a sky shame reddens like a sting
None of his questions will wait for any answer
And noon is self-slain before night's reckoning

[Translated by BABETTE DEUTSCH]

118

JEAN SANS TERRE THE ASSASSIN

John leaves the city of the Tantalids
Where human glances cast an evil spell
He takes the olive-tree in his valise
The secret of the king in his golden eyes

He saves the voice of the sunken fountain
And the unknown brother of his mirror
The nights of storm have not thundered in vain
Although his youth was throttled in a drawer

The forgers have burnished the dawn
The glaziers have refurnished the yesterdays
The world is still rich with Eleonores
His heart must break the record of the time

He steals the egg of the eagle and the phoenix
The grains of heaven and the stars of earth
But his flesh remains hungry without pride
He eats the bird without digesting the flight

He dances to the terror of the candles
He sings to the old silence of the mountains
His crown crashes to the potter's field
While his blue flower twines at the feet of the gallows

When he arrives at the Hotel with a cracked heart
He meets at last the queen of the chimera
At dawn he will kill her with a sneer
And leave his worn-out self at the checkroom

[*Translated by* KENNETH PATCHEN]

JOHN WITHOUT A COUNTRY BUT NOT WITHOUT MYSTERY

The full moon stirs a chlorine bath
To burn me like a poisoned well
I drink at springs of phosphorus
The nothingness the unknown spell

A sleeper in the smothered city
I wander through haunted chateaux
Whose broken glassy windows stare
Where the forgotten lover goes

I stumble past the fallen columns
That once held up the roof of times
Amidst their ruins my upright column
Of bones and shadows grows and climbs

And waits till in the mines of silence
The cry of cries has ripened and grown
And pierces through the night of trance
Where my pale sleep rots overthrown

My weary and neurotic shadow
Risen out of the den of fear
Remembering that she is my sister
She leans over me and tries to cheer

Without Earth—yet not without mystery
Without Earth—yet not terrorless
Under my coat of mammifer
An angel waits that I confess

Deep in the dullest galleries
In my old body's misery
Beneath the sweats and cavities
The very God habits with me

Without land? Without mystery too
Without Graal and Baal and law and faith
I'll be the poorest on the earth
As long as I don't loose my Self

Crow perched upon my spine: my friend
With beak that living flesh must feel
Cleanse every shadow from my bones
Be more ferocious than bare steel

O take away my eager flesh
And take my subterranean dream
Take me from me! And over all
That human hope that still may gleam

[Translated by JOHN GOULD FLETCHER]

THE SACRIFICE OF
JEAN SANS TERRE

Landless, without a roof upon
The roads of earth, poet whose wail
Is miserere, John achieves the last wharves
Where one takes ship for Nothing and sets sail

To the landlords they have apportioned earth
For the lucky with dice the heavens rest
Landless belongs to all of earth
And the possessor is possessed

If he transports a morsel of clay
From north to south from here to there
Why he would cover his mother away
Dead in a ground that is God's share

Let exhaustion have worn him down
Used up even memory to devour
Him like saltpeter he has known
The petals of a self unfold its flower

He the most shambling of mammals, most
Despoiled of all the angels is
He is starving with a panther's fast
The longing of a saint upon his knees

His vigor of hunger to crush
Himself sets the pyre ablaze
He is burning the deception of flesh
Away—for your nearness, haze.

He feels the void's draft; weight falls
To ethereal zero and freed
Avid, the flesh disenthralls
He is Jupiter's son and his seed.

[*Translated by* LÉONIE ADAMS]

JEAN SANS TERRE'S MARCH

(First Version)

John Landless marches marches
Marches on his ancient land

His heart beats beats beats
And he cannot stop his feet

Neither the hills nor the crests
On the Earth make him rest

Neither dust of desert areas
Nor the tender primaveras

John Landless wears out the earth
Like he wears out his soles

Yet the heels of his boots
Wear out stone-quartz and roots

Wear out Smyrna's wool
Wear out ruins' marble

Over roads of black asphalt
Over roads of bitter salt

Neither the pains of his tumors
Nor the pools of his sweat

Nor the ticks nor the thorns
In his skin make him quit

He eats birds and grasses
He drinks from streams he passes

He cloaks himself in sunlight
To cross the Sahara at night

Ever marching forward
He fights with the wind's heart

Marching at random on this earth
Toward the end of the universe

[Translated by ERIC SELLIN]

JEAN SANS TERRE'S MARCH

(Second Version)

Landless John tramps tramps
Tramps across the old earth stamps
On the skull of his mother clamps
On the bright-hearted primulas

Landless John tramps tramps
And his bootsole creaks creaks
Crossing the chimera's track
And where brackish dust is thick

Landless John wears out the earth
Wears out the pebbles granite too
Wears out the hobnails in his shoe
Wears out his thigh bone and his thew

Landless John tramps tramps
Over bridges under arches
Over asphalt roads he marches
Under clouds of dews and damps

Stumblingly he goes he tumbles
In the mire through the briars
With the blood of tumors wet
Dabbled with his salty sweat

How move on how stay alive
In the vineyards ever dry
Starved for bread among the rye
And his loins heavy with love?

Landless John tramps on tramps on
His skeleton is creaking creaking
His heart clip-clop is beating beating
Suddenly it will stop

[Translated by BABETTE DEUTSCH]

125

JEAN SANS TERRE
LEADS THE CARAVAN

Have I a hundred years since or
A hundred thousand tramped these wastes
With a track more vulnerable
Than fire of a sun that hastes?

My camel leads the caravan
Through centuries of rusted sand
To find as might any profane wind
The key to the oblivion land

My great grandparents long since
Have worked this sea and no less
Could their passing shadow have brought
To yoke the ancient nothingness

Although life's mortal light
Would wring their hearts about by day
Still they had a candle lit
For antique love to find the way

In me their ancient skeleton
Of gold calcined by the years
And my new flesh tries as it may
To fill it with heavy cares

I hear the red wolf that howls
On the cavern of my blood
Cracking the bones at nightfall
Of the dream again abroad

Sail on sail on slow dromedaries
And traverse eternity
From the quaternary dawns
To the tomb's near certainty

My kin with limbs of gold and ebony
Die of thirst and of hope the most
At both my wrists I open the veins
That may prove to them a host

I wish that my love would rot
And never see light again
If by this final sacrifice
A young god be born in men

If without Alp to water
From the desert's lifeless skin
The freshness of a rose should rise
And a cloak of sudden green

No bitch will I need to chase
The hunger of a jackal
Enough that my faith revive
And the aurora of my choral

Offering those who covet
Slow camel and proud lion
Salt from my weak moist hand
The strength of my religion

[Translated by WILLIAM CARLOS WILLIAMS]

JEAN SANS TERRE
TAKES HIS BATH OF BLOOD

I stride the dawn and far and wide bespatter
With blood the trembling gardens startled wood
My head is pure but O my shadow's red
That thickens dark the pools of blood

My feet I bathe in smoke-exhaling tides
Of purple wrapped around the ocean's shore
The amaranthine moon's enflowered foam
Shall serve as my shampoo of perfumed gore

O blood! O blood! O food supreme
Red as the rain that is the desert milk
And red the spring that gushing from our wounds
Pours up to hell aflame as scarlet silk

Upon my old cathedrals blood shall rain
While seas of crimson rise and overbrim
The eagle's wing and the shark's fin
Shall drag us to the world's infernal rim

An all-red bull in whom a god's incarnate
Shall stop by lick my clover white and green
His thick slow blood shall flow to swell our Marnes
And thrust our destinies down void obscene

Near slaughterhouses let me browse and sip
Baptismal waters that one time were mine
The gravid taurine wine shall tilt my brain
And keep me drunk till I with death combine

Then brooding I shall bear the mammal's cry
Whose eye's transformed into a saturn sun
A brother lessons me to suffer wrong
And evil all-invading as the hun

The hatching mouth of memories I kiss
And strive to pacify the wolf with sleep
The traitor mouth that's like Vesuvius
Of which no love can dam the yawning deep

Encamped so stolid in my cheater-heart
My butcher's hand shall soon betray the brute
My mad excesses cannot long be hid
Beneath my blood-crowned hat and brow hirsute

From every pore my blood drips drips
And infiltrates my trace in sand wind flood
Where Landless John in flight has passed this way
You shall be told by his long trail of blood

[Translated by GEORGE REAVEY]

JEAN SANS TERRE GOES TO WAR

(Remembering "Marlborough S'en Va-t-en Guerre")

Off to the war now Landless goes
With a hey-nonny-no nonny-no
Off to the war now Landless goes
And why he does God only knows
And why he does God only knows
And why he does God only knows

He marches off to the boundaries
With a hey nonny-no nonny-no
But there's nothing there but rocks and trees
There's nothing there but rocks and trees
There's nothing there but rocks and trees

On a cushion of fern John Landless lies
With a hey nonny-no nonny-no
And under the bindwood lifts his eyes
To sweep the empty country skies
And seek in vain his enemies

He once had thought all men were good
With a hey nonny-no nonny-no
He though they lived in brotherhood
As men and women naturally would
Sharing their burdens and their food

But then the government one day
With a hey nonny-no nonny-no
Decided he had to go away
And leave his parents one fine day
And leave them there until doomsday

Mrs. John Landless lovely wife
With a hey nonny-no nonny-no
Somewhere leading a quiet life
Begins to despair of her husband's life
As she waits for the mail each day of her life

In the sky above the white doves soar
With a hey nonny-no nonny-no
The meadows are thick with buttercups
A bomb comes down a bird flies up
And Landless is no more

Mrs. John Landless now you know
With a hey nonny-no nonny-no
Your husband is a great hero
He has found his land so let him go
And please don't keep on weeping so

[Translated by WILLIAM JAY SMITH]

JEAN SANS TERRE
THROWS HIMSELF ON THE STEPS
OF STRASBOURG CATHEDRAL

Immaculate
Love's cathedral
The returnless' great
Last port of call

While far, bell-sown
Time's seed is spent
Awaits me in stone
Thine angel's ascent

Thou risen to ponder
Ten centuries so
The white-lit thunder
The circling crow

Wheat-ear, out of stone
Towering, of sweat
Supplication
Fervour beget

That thou art turned rose
And translation alone
Of spirit all blows
Of thy gardens grown

Shoot and slip
Prospered fair
In thee who dost dip
Up faith Rhine-pure

Hopfields', vines'
Daughter, wilt snare
Of horizons, signs
Taller than before

Springing always
With red-blondes of
A new day's
Dawn in love

So to be filled
As full moons pass
With riches; old golds
Twilighted to amass

The meadows' topmast
Prime barley shoot
Nobody downcast
Thou hast forgot

Now at thy porch
I kneel, bow head
Thee to besmirch
With peccavis said

In thy portals keep
Stretch me breath'd rank
With garlic for sleep
The same whose drink

Was, times since
Red grenadine, he
Who would steal pears once
From the cloister tree

Wan brother, walked
The roads, their sad
Friar so abject
The dogs fled

Such scurvy slips
To thy folds to hide
Look my palm drips
Christ's blood who died

133

And I crave this
Again for my peace
Great Milady caress
Of thy mild kiss

[*Translated by* LÉONIE ADAMS]

JOHN THE FIRE

I have set fire to the forest of my ancestors
I have brought back the proud and unavowed Flame
The daughter of liberty that I saw born
Of an ancient mountain and young thunder

Native of Asia pupil of Heraclitus
I have reintroduced her to the house of the Fathers
Where since thy departure the Tree of the Law exhausts itself
And unknowing pyres prepare their anger

And I have made her dance before the tabernacle
Where the ancient oaks grow under their moss
My feline Fire my Teller of Oracles
Has refilled the past with her red breath

Mad fire! High mass or disaster
The artist skilfully lights its spirals
From the wood of old branch-lines shaking on surveyed lands
The flames of the most instantaneous cathedral rise

The flying buttresses of ancient maples
The towers of Charity raised in suffering
The deer carrying their antlers like candelabra
And the golden bees sown in mosaics

The transepts the towers tormented with crows
Traversed by foxes grilled in their fur
Jacob's ladder suddenly breaks and totters
And the surprised angels have burning wings

[Translated by LOUISE BOGAN]

135

JOHN THE ORCHESTRA LEADER

A thunder of silence
Demented lover, I draw
My cruel substance
From your pure element

Oh from my solitude
Surges, young potion,
The credo of preludes
The first emotion

I declare my war
On eternal sleep
I devastate all shores
With fire and sleet

I launch my storms
On the mahogany forest
And I wrench sacred beasts
From the lairs where they rest

With a finger I uproot
The oaks of Apollo
The sugars of resins
From the violins flow

I raise up stones
With a magic round
And make them lighter
Than a calm sea's sound

Shattered asphalts
Yawning sapphires—
Forgetting exults
At the sound of my zephyrs

And from the brass age
Springs the ancient fate
The darting bee which
The first dawns intoxicate

Oh violoncellos
Obese like human hearts
The burden of your sorrows
Pervades all my parts

With the shock of my trumpets
I rattle down Jericho
And the watchman Death
Flees at the echo

With the shafts of my arms
I prop up the skies
And the ethers resound
With the enchantment of my cries

Oh flute kind companion
Of pure memory's fire
Melt the mountain the canyon
And their somber desire

But with my sweet harp
I shall calm your nerves
Crowd sad and compact
Filling the universe

Men, from your viscera
I extract the despair
Impure, you are now free
Of your lies and black cares

From your wide-gaping sores
I make a voice rise
Human warm and true:
Christ's plaint to the skies

[*Translated by* Eric Sellin]

JOHN THE RIVER

River without a Land, ohé! John Landless' course
The waters do not choose between the banks but flow
Onward between those rivals mutually bound
East-West, the Yes-and-No, the youthful and the slow

Does he adjudicate between the hush, the cries?
He who knows well the springs' gestation underground
Asks of the winds a vote of confidence, will trace
The figure of the flight on which the birds are bound

Rightward he views the aging walls of Nineveh
And ancient kings who fling their rubies to the base
And sees the powerful palace betray itself at last
And the descending rain displume proud Samothrace

Upon the other shore he sees the Amazons
Plunge freely where the cunning billow braves
Their large frank eyes, enriched with belladonna, keen
To pierce the ancient secret of the incestuous waves

Fishers and riverfolk will stand before their huts
To watch the river flow, not jealous of his glory
Let him seek out the spirit in regions far from here
If they may fish and drink and beach a loaded dory

River without a Land, its wave ephemeral
Down to the sea it flows, no choice, no faltering
Between peace on the right and war upon the left
From dawn quick with desire to dusk remembering

[*Translated by* Babette Deutsch]

138

JEAN SANS TERRE IS LANDSICK

Across five continents
My prostrate body lies
All of my capitals
Utter the same cries

Dark names of towns where fear
Prowls in the market place
Speak to the ages
Of our hearts' disgrace

Sun of melinite
At dawn I am afraid
To hear your bombshell sputter
In subterranean shade

And when the moon climbs high
On balconies of light
Our death is scented by
Its lily of dynamite

Is this my heart that sounds?
Is this my pulse that beats?
I ache in Barcelona
In Guernica's red streets

My feet touch China where
The dying children stood
In Palestine my forehead
Blushes with young blood

I ache in my old oaks
Downed by the fusillade
Depriving the dull plains
Of their paternal shade

Drawing by Eugene Berman

Oh tell me in what tongue
I can sing now unwanted
Words are exhausted
And the spirit haunted

Under what minaret
In what cathedral spire
Must I inter my cymbals
My secret and desire

Death prowls the stricken land
And roars across the sky
Silent in my retreat
Of whitened bones I lie

Oh I am landsick as
The animal that must
Hatch out the ancestral sob
In its nocturnal dust

[Translated by CLARK MILLS]

JEAN SANS TERRE'S RACE

(First Version)

Landless John runs the Marathon
Against his shadow under the outrage of sun
He narrows rivers distorts meridians
He walks the endless highways of Tartarus

He quits the poisonous solitude of cities
He quits the crowd with insane glottis
Wears out the wheel of earth the tires of wind
His knees grind the rust of sunsets and dawns

He wears the magical shoes of every desire
The seven-league boots that cover Achilles' heel
He wears the skin of calf lamb buffalo antelope
Crushes the rock of silence the goblins of recollection

At the Pont-Neuf he crosses the river of fate
He bends and begs the waters that veer beyond
To wash the mask from his unknown face
To rinse the blue fear from his sagging brow

He asks the mirror if he will arrive on time
On time no matter where nowhere
He unties the strings of his old smile
And tries to rub the lifeline from his palms

From every bridge he feeds the little fishes
Crumbs of his bread flow to the Jordan
Lees of his sad wine to the Guadalquivir
Stalactites of his tears hang in the Dniester

He throws the gold of magi in the Nile
The slumber of poppies in the Yang-Tze
Feathers from his dream in the Amazon
The ashes of the beloved in the Seine

From week to week he goes from market to market
Monday to the flower-wedding
Tuesday to the horse and bird-fair
Wednesday to the copper-boom

Thursday he sells the bear-skin
Friday he buys God's grace
Saturday-love at bargain prices
Withers in the rain of Sundays

John stops at the hotels of insomnia
He calls at rotisseries of prime beef
At bars where oblivion sells by the quart
At cafés where he meets the unknown woman

On Veronica's breast he hears the knell of disaster
From Mary's lips he steals the cosmic lie
He meets his ancestor in Rachel's eye
But Liliane's love bakes him the loaf of life

He goes he goes—and dogs bark in his flesh
From their spires the cities watch him go
The countryside blushes with flowers when he comes near
The earth is in love with Landless John

He is the fence for all earthly goods
He owns cotton corn wool lead ruby
But he took a mortgage on the Upanishads
He pays the tithe to the gods under the Aeschylean code

He suffers the death of the thousand quattrocento Christs
He wears the toppers of every human reason
Helmet beret tiara sombrero cap straw and silk hat
For marriages christenings polo-games cock-fights funerals

But one evening he stops
He stands no longer on his galvanized feet
He is no longer the lightning rod
Vertical between earth's sleep and heaven's wrath

He has lost the race with his shadow
He is stretched out on the mattress of the thousand spines
Soon he will feed the spider with his dreams
The millstone of the earth grinds his rattle

[*Translated by* LIONEL ABEL]

JEAN SANS TERRE'S RACE

(Second Version)

John Landless walks the world over
On staked out roads of abattoirs
On bony pavements of memory
On sands sculptured by a virgin wind

He walks in the jealous mud of the deluge
On foot-paths under the apple-trees of love
On the slag of fields of defeat
On boulevards washed with human tears

> John Landless walks walks
> His shoes go clack clack
> His bones crack crack
> And the earth turns turns

But the sole of his foot never takes root
His thieving toes do not cling to any rock
His metatarsal bones crumble like hollow columns
His tendons hammer out the rhythm of the will in vain

His knees become naked along the length of roads
The muscles of his thighs unbend under the suction of marshes
The muscles of his legs are dislocated like old rubber-bands
His joints grind with the rust of fatigue

> John Landless walks walks
> His shoes go clack clack
> His bones crack crack
> And the earth turns turns

His foot is more sensitive to the pits of mystery
Than the ring of the sorcerer or the instruments of the geologist
He knows the melancholy expectation of schists
And the impatient revolt of basalts

He knows the childish smile of flints
The useless call of waste land
The complaints of marshes and the sighs of moss
The cries of valleys that sleep with shadow

> John Landless walks walks
> His shoes go clack clack
> His bones crack crack
> And the earth turns turns

He walks even as far as the suburbs of peoples' hunger
Even to the end of the road of thirst
Even to the summit where total glory consumes itself
Even to the mouths of degraded rivers

He walks under the gaze of a tyrant sun
Under the filmy cascade of the moon
He passes by the orchards of sadistic rain
And leans upon the crutches of the friendly wind

> John Landless walks walks
> His shoes go clack clack
> His bones crack crack
> And the earth turns turns

He stops at each bridge to renew himself
He leans over the water to change his looks
To rinse fear from his temples
And scratch the tartar of his despair

He walks over bridges of all the ages
Bridges of every contradiction
From the left bank to the right bank
From yes to no from justice to injustice

> John Landless walks walks
> His shoes go clack clack
> His bones crack crack
> And the earth turns turns

146

Ponte Vecchio Pont Neuf
Puente Alcarante Benkei Bashi
Pons Augustus Teufelsbrücke
Pont des Morts Brooklyn Bridge

From the height of bridges he feeds little fishes
The crumbs of his bread float toward the Jordan
The lees of his sad wine toward Quadalquivir
The stalactites of his tears drop into the Volga

Still farther he walks and still more he loves his journey
The four winds dart to pursue him
The five continents open to him the deltas of their harbors
The seven oceans encircle him

> John Landless walks walks
> His shoes go clack clack
> His bones crack crack
> And the earth turns turns

[Translated by LOUISE BOGAN]

JEAN SANS TERRE
CIRCLES THE EARTH SEVEN TIMES

At blond dawn
A life unfurled
He journeys far
To the great world

He departs alone
The mystery soldier
A simple flower
In his button-hole

Smiling always
Blinking clear
He deceives love
At each frontier

In the cities
Boiling with beer
All gaiety
Loses its cheer

At the port bars
Watched for his grace
The strong boys
Hate his face

Beloved by the seas
And fever isles
Bitter winds
Kiss him whiles

Seven times
He circles the earth
Bearing his faith
In his head's girth

Barber bootblack
Priest corsair
Emperor bankrupt
Wastrel's fair

It's small matter
The world to course
To eat fire
To make wars

Oh the same trouble
Everywhere
Coming and going
Walk and stair

Morning and night
Bread and thirst
Flesh and dream
Here! Eat and burst!

Individual
Sad heart and bare
Wordless and nameless
His own despair

No papers left
No heirs found
Beg for your death
At the burying-ground

[Translated by WILLIAM CARLOS WILLIAMS]

JEAN SANS TERRE
BRAVES THE TEMPEST

Thus John one day
Sails from the shore
Upon the good ship
"Nevermore"

Green with scum
Caked with salt
Her course is laid
For the heavenly vault

She sails forever
And a day
Even her anchor
Is washed away

The sky on fire
The sea in flight
John the drunkard
Remains upright

Under the wind's whip
Swinging free
He laughs and spits
Into the sea

"Despite the rage
You cannot spend
O brother storm
I am your friend

Your wings beat out
A weighty message
I seek for combat
Be its presage

Ventriloquist sea
Gulp down my heart
And pound this hull
Till it falls apart

And damn my eyes
Since I can lose
Nothing but this
Enormous nose

I've had enough
Of this dead pan
Carry me under
If you can!"

A man of courage
With his two hands
John shakes the sky
From where he stands

But suddenly
The tempest clears
And over his head
The day appears

And John who brandished
Fist in air
Falls back again
To his despair

[Translated by CLARK MILLS]

JEAN SANS TERRE
FECUNDATES THE SEA

Rear you and toss my mare, the unsurpassed
Noble-nostrilled, nacreous-eyed, this slight
Cockle set to quivering keel and mast
With your blazings' and your surges' might

My mast shall surmount headlong sea
Your ill-nature, bland to lewdness, to excess
Unheeding, I will knight it gallantly
Through the last vagaries of blue womaness

Before the sweep of your imperial
Foam, sham granites, puny leads, and sweep
Of any metal that lies in your swart will
The fiddlestrings of my nerves will not snap

My whole passion moves breathless to fulfill
Parting me lip from lip incessantly
Updrawn, wave fervid, receding that will
Bride me and exhaust with every sigh

Your milks I churn, I whip to foam your creams
Tokays, Bordeaux I have stirred up your wines
I have poured in one the liqueurs of the extremes
And am the hopeless drunkard of your brines

I knead your ferments and your yeasts to be
My loaf I shape of a sea-batter and from
Your broths arisen of lava and mercury
The one whose prophecy is tomorrow comes

And I roam your cities where the chimeras dwell
Sounding of bells the deep-sea divers bring
Along their streets precipitous and chill
Where you have set the polyps laboring

But you are mother soon, and milder, sea
And all the fountaining sally you constrain
Of your prime being, and give for brevity
Of love translation in the womb's hard pain

You brood on the young days of sardines and keep
The decorum of tunas in solicitude
Upholding the constitution of the deep
Or else the bad would swallow up the good

The venom of the rascasse dose out to him
And oil the agilities of the sturgeon's bones
Let pass the whale the scavenger to sweep trim
The burial places of the littler ones

Forgotten soon enough the sailor he
Whose hunt is pursued aloft, upon a ground
That's starred. You careen no more and languidly
But touch in the end a wrist the sun has tanned

Yet in your widowhood one day it may be
—Twisting forsaken sheets and frenzying then—
Will sound for you the turbines' monody
And it will bear to you the name of man

[Translated by Léonie Adams]

153

JEAN SANS TERRE
CROSSES THE ATLANTIC

At last it fails and falls away in dust
That land of so much fear and crumbled stone
Old Europe's pantheons are but a crust
A nameless cape a ragged heap of bone

And now no longer on the antique shores
Will one pursue the stars of love he lost
The golden kursaals and the useless stores
Of sentiment are permanently closed

O sea-whore garmented in lace of foam
Why do you draw me down into your bed
The coverlets of mist cold as the tomb
Where coral grows that richest blood has fed?

From deep in gardens rich with iodine
You watch with longing any clumsy mate
Who drunken with your salty emerald wine
Might waken the old shudders you await

The naked drowned who plunge to your demesnes
And through whose ribs the silver sturgeon swim
Their guts alive and wriggling with sardines
Come down to love you winged like cherubim

I captain of your sea-horse squadron will
Command your deserts and your hidden dreams
I plant my masts on every waving hill
And slumber calmly on your nervous streams

In vain you summon me with glittering face
And with the chemical power of your eyes
My bolted armor balks your false embrace
My ears are sealed against your drunken sighs

Do you regret the feast of Salamis?
The red banquet at the Armada's blast?
Fond of blue admirals your precipice
Yawns always greedy for a new repast

But see the sodden leaking hulls that teem
With passengers escaped from Tartarus
Who bring with their dust and imperfect dream
To Thalatta the earthy tetanus

More bent and bowed than the Atrides ever
Fleeing the stolid hatred of the cliffs
Abjuring their belief and their endeavor
They seek the ocean's vaulted caves and drifts

They are the black pox they are the chimera
They are the plague because they are the mind
And have been vomited by the bitter era
Because they are too wise and too resigned

I weighed their scepters and I took their crutches
I knew their nightmares and I saw their sweat
I watched their daughters whom the reaper touches
Their old men's fear I shall not soon forget

Adopt and comfort all this landless host
Who own no sprig of thyme nor leaf of cress
Nor trunk nor stove nor lark nor cloud nor ghost
Nor even the small tree of loneliness

Oh welcome all this flotsam of the lands
Leave for an instant your proud lovers' kiss
And be with waves changed into arms and hands
The errants' anxious mother and abyss

[Translated by CLARK MILLS]

JEAN SANS TERRE LANDS

Landing, in the destroying lands; put in
At wry America, at entrances
Giving on nowhere of rotted harbors again
My last bet lost and lost my Parises

The breed of fog the fog will breed my death
I drink fog in strong draughts of liquor eat
Of the fog its soup and sidedish swath
Me in fog from callouses to throat

Always to re-enact old wretchedness
With its beard trailing the six thousand years
Its beard of the Phoenician cut I use
To wipe away an evil season's tears

Wary of the railway agony I was thus
With the hangars' melancholy imbrued
Christ is dead now, I am no Lazarus
Against the zinc of bars the nickels thud

Flight too become no longer worth one's while
You can move on at ease, continually
Crossing meridians and not find the isle
That used to offer you the future free

And all the ships Epiphany set sail
The ones with the auroral cargoes come
Unloading only their unseasonable
Fruits still too bitter and some casks of scum

Their menace once, the raging eye of rule
Armoured cars of the whirlwind I'd butt at
With a laugh—I mustered that—and the bare skull
But retain all the terror of a rat

This is the stockade at which I tear
The wall of walls no end of it until
My ailment of a shadow dogs me where
One goes on down to the lowest thing of all

I have been deafened now to the bitch-whines
To the buffalo yearnings of ancestral tones
One sound alone deep, deep in time complains
As if a mattock rasped upon my bones

[*Translated by* LÉONIE ADAMS]

JEAN SANS TERRE SINGS AN ODE TO FRANCE IN MAY 1940

(First Version)

France a first communicant
Child of Mary and of May
In your village smelling of mint
The angel and the criminal loved you

Were you not the fiancée
Of landless people everywhere
Daughter of flesh and of thought
More chaste than the briar-rose?

Did you not have your fine empire
From Paris to Madagascar
Where you could take your deliriums for walks
And caress the leopard?

But behind your curtain of barley
Where the lark sharpens the air
Did you never hear the forges
And the growls of Fafnir?

And under your armor fashioned by Rude
Did you not feel your breasts shiver
Pointing toward the coarse hand
Raving to be imprisoned?

Jeanne d'Arc gentle peasant
Seduced by the Sleeping Beauty's wood
The sons of your Rhenish loves
Will realise punishment

Kneeling in your fields of strawberries
Crucified on your espaliered trees
Over all the land of France
Pours your spring-time blood

And the fisherman on the bank of the Oise
Gathering up his catch
Will no longer lead his woman
Among the rushes to make love

The sky suddenly darkens with eagles
Laying their eggs at evening
Your warrior lying in the wheat
Does not know that he is a hero

And in the parallel fields
Where the angelus has not rung
Fingernails teeth and eyeballs
Will be harvested in summer

Neither Bruges nor Rouen nor Chartres
Have enough angels in their towers
To struggle against these hawks
And these troops of vultures

Nous n'irons plus au bois ma belle
Les lauriers sont coupés les ponts
Adieu Cadet Rousselle
Au revoir Pont d'Avignon

The dead embrace the silence
Of a century which will bring them revenge
O France you rhyme with sufferance
Your song will never come to silence

[Translated by Louise Bogan]

159

JEAN SANS TERRE SINGS AN ODE TO FRANCE IN MAY 1940

(Second Version)

Nous n'irons plus au bois ma belle
Les lauriers sont coupés les ponts
And the rainbows are cut down as well
And even the Pont d'Avignon

Mortal statue Joan of Arc
Only a piece of bloodstained bronze
In this silent land of France
Your heart too has ceased its songs

Joan sits in her homespun skirt
By the bushes of raspberry
She prepares a rich red jam
With the blood of cavalry

The black hen of the clouds
Lays the rotten eggs of death
The plucked village cocks foretell
Winds blowing from the north

For dawn has a leaden wing
And the sun is but a shell
Which levels the roadside lilies
As well as the citadel

The sky of France is black
With lemures and crows
They do not know they are heroes
Who crouch in the hedgerows

Too few are the angels of stone
At Chartres at Reims at Beauvais
To fight off the oncoming flood
The squadrons of birds of prey

Bull chased from the pasture
And the silence of his sires
Loses his blood in sunlight
Before the outrage of purple fires

He loses his blood by fountains
By his brooks by his veins
By his spouts by his nostrils
By the Oise by the Aisne

The twelve sisters of his rivers
Undo with a crooked motion
The slipknots of their shoelaces
And hurl themselves in the ocean

Drink drink you drunken warriors
The sour blood of Burgundy
The fermented wine of fear
The brandy of calamity

The country overflows with tears
Welling up from every door
Eau-de-vie is dead water now
You will drink it more and more

Nous n'irons plus au bois ma belle
Les lauriers sont coupés les ponts
And the rainbows are cut down as well
And even the Pont d'Avignon

[Translated by ROBERT WERNICK]

JEAN SANS TERRE SINGS THE BALLAD OF ALL MOTHERS

At all the world's windows
The shades are drawn tight
A mother in mourning
Speaks to the angel of night

Speaks to the angel of night
Of her son gone to war
She plays over a prayer
On the harp of her heart

On the harp of her heart
Each mother plays
An old schoolboy tune
She remembers school days

She remembers school days
Above the empty bed
The same picture is hung
From Moscow to Madrid

From Kladno to Quimper
He could throw his ball
Farthest of all the boys
From Antwerp to Mobile

From Belgrade to Tiflis
He now throws a grenade
Look at the fireworks!
Goodbye fair maids!

Goodbye fair maids!
In the streets of Changsha
In the streets of Odessa
It's all crosses now!

It's all crosses now!
And watching all night
At all the world's windows
The little mothers sit

The little mothers sit
Without sleep or sound
They rock their sons on the sea
They hide them underground

They hide them underground
While they listen alone
To the whistle of the trains
That will never come home

That will never come home?
But I heard someone say
That war will soon die!
You will kill it my boy!

You will kill it my boy
My hero my son
My angel my lover
My baby my man

My baby my man
Don't press me so tight
The fruit-trees are in flower
My heart is full of night!

[Translated by Robert Wernick]

JEAN SANS TERRE
STROLLS DOWN BROADWAY

One hundred and thirty stories, haunt of the Danaides
Nests of a merciless solitude
A people wedged tight in its chrysalis
Not knowing why it's part of this neighborhood

For all these people who divide the Earth
In brazen provinces and fields of grain
Don't they realize they are landless men
Cowering under oblivion's reign?

One hundred and thirty empty stories
Resounding with calls but never hearing
Despite the anger of the telephones
The world turns on turns on unstopping

Throbbing walls of progressive days
Historic fat of the Bowery
Where a graveyard of pioneers lies
And rots beneath the pantings of dark kitchen-ways

None of these walls are alive with murmurs
They vibrate alone to the cry of death's lance
Under the incrusted smile of phantoms
The heart declines the kisses of chance

Under this Broadway of spittle and mud
Leaps the crazed herd of the subway
The last beasts eager for each other's blood
Screaming the dolorous cries of the *heimweh*

All bronze is hollow and all marble fake
About these tin-foil battlements
You lean out over treacherous cliffs to take
In your arms the cosmic elements

And all the gold deep in the mountains
The deadened sun of sterilized fire
Will soon be but a stagnant mire
The dung of an eagle tamed on the winds

This gold has not revealed its birth
And man goes back to sleep in peace
Abandoned to the powers of Earth
Suspended above forgetting's abyss.

[Translated by Eric Sellin]

JEAN SANS TERRE
PURCHASES MANHATTAN

Manhattan Rock: phantom of vertical clay
Whose welcome greets the ship far off the coast
Before thy bankers and thy longshoremen
I lift my ancient hat a threadbare ghost

Kissed by the ocean thy inhuman Alp
Rises from those in sweat of labor drowned
Alp where the voiceless herds of sorrow graze
Where springs of soda gush from underground

And on the Hudson the red ferries wander
Like the swift shuttles driven by the weaver
Who weaves into his ancient tapestry
Figures that fade and melt into the river

But here old age like twilight comes more swiftly
Grass withers and the iron grows brown with stain
A hundred stories clothe the void
Solitude calls her sister but in vain

Close your accounts: boom years of the twenties
Drive from the Bowery all who are forgotten
Beneath the innocent giants of the earth
The graves of the rabbies lie rotten

The turnstile in the subway grinds the crowd
The paper pulp the pulp of destiny
The crowd that like a flood of sperm disperses
And scatters towards the beds of infamy

And at Times Square the merchants of the storm
Sell the split fifes and drums of death and offer
The candelabra of the festival
Insurance benefits for those who suffer

166

Take out a mortgage against human wisdom
Lease the suburban greensward in the Park
The Fates in combine purchase shares of cotton
The stock-exchange of irony is closed and dark

If man climbs to the peak of Jacob's ladder
And smiles down from the hundred-second story
He stumbles down the staircase of old age
Towards Job's poor bone-yard far from fame and glory

Sell death buy the Eumenides
Sell wind sell liberty
Buy dream sell the Hebrides
Oh sell and buy and sell and sell and buy

I buy Manhattan for a single smile
I sell it back for immortality
Some day this white sand will no longer glisten
The rock will dream of a forgotten city

[Translated by CLARK MILLS]

JEAN SANS TERRE
ON THE BOWERY

The bark of Charon lands in Fulton Market
Full of human spines and fish-heads
To fertilize famished cemeteries

The men are disguised as divers
For the struggle in the depths of fogs
Their electric eyes spit blood and ink

Tons of lemons cascade from the Lackawanna freight cars
Almond trees descend the Ihpetonga highway
In the middle of Union Square a leper colony explodes

In the little hotels of the Bowery madness ferments
The green eyes of their windows
Reflect immemorial holocausts

Ulysses of Scyros! Shepherds of Tyre! Merchants of Gomor-
    rah!
Reduced to nothing in your dog-huts
Ornamented with spitoons carpeted with sighs

Hear the sobs of the ventiloquial night
The sleepers in the morgue are not at ease
What crime reddens the hands of the dawn?

[*Translated by* LOUISE BOGAN]

JEAN SANS TERRE
SALUTES THE HARLEM RIVER

This water this black alcohol that draws us on
This white whiskey where black eyes are swimming
These sulphurous pools where black flies are flowering
These green dragons and black dragons of the plague

O sorrowful wave
White dance black dance red dance yellow dance
Dance of all the seas that give suck as one breast
Massacre of all mothers that choke as one throat
                Harlem! Black priestess
                  Drunk on the white milk of the dew

O river with mole-colored hair
And a scintillant girdle of salmon russet steel
Chaldean dancer in this dirty hole of America
Pinning a moon of gold between your filthy breasts
Toward you descend the cats of our flesh
And the reflexions of our shattered sheet-iron

O ancient wave
Wave of the yellow Tiger and of pitchy Harlem
My pillow is stuffed with the scales of cheap fish
Sad wave overwhelmed
By so many drowned heads
Somber river which defies the ocean
With its sluices of death

                      [Translated by BABETTE DEUTSCH]

JEAN SANS TERRE
DISCOVERS THE WEST POLE

John Landless leads his landless folk
All those who owned no window and no door
And nothing but the bed to die and to be born
And the shadowy bitch licking their misery

They wander on the roads of centuries
Riding the meager mare of hope
Seething with the yellow fever of the night
Feeding on black milk and bitter herbs

They leave the upright house in the godless street
Stores of oblivion factories of ghosts
They even leave the blooming tree of knowledge
On which are hung their brothers and their fears

Although they know the codes of human reasons
And touch the antic oxen at their tail
And grasp the trout at the garnet ear
And value fur and pulp and fat

They go ahead harassed by the tempest's fury
By glowing snow and by the wind of myth
Chased by the trumpets of the Scythian wrath
And by the blizzard of sharp whetted eyes

John Landless led them out of time and doubt
Out of the iron cities and the Pharaoh towers
Out of the depths and oblique corridors
Along the heedless roads

A gray-haired angel took them to the hill
Offering them the conquest of the Western Pole
The moon-bird flew and dropped his golden feathers
Over the dust of waking centuries

Here the landless folk will build Westopolis
Again stores of oblivion factories of ghosts
Again the upright houses down the godless street
And trees of knowledge where friends are hanged

John Landless flees at dawn back toward East alone

[*Translated by* WILLIAM CARLOS WILLIAMS]

JEAN SANS TERRE IN CUBA

Here then are the final republics
Islands of sweet vanity
Where they share the public orange
And freedom slowly grows old

Here are the islands of nonchalance
The Final West where glory falls asleep
Man rots under the tree of luck
Dying of hunger under lemons of gold

Under anicent ceibas the centaurs camp
Reduced by homo sapiens to beg
And they offer to the pyres of the dawn
The sweetness of their almond maidens

Little girls of impenetrable sorrow
Twenty thousand trembling Semiramises
Burn up at thirteen their quiet youth
To feed a family of ten

In the suburbs a people of panthers
Holds out a bronze hook and a copper eye
To break the dams of poverty
And cut through invisible knots

But betraying the impatience of a century
The people drink the moon that tastes of rum
And in the daring rhythm of the rhumba
They prepare the forum-drums

Meanwhile havanas are being smoked
And the desires of this world are undone
The brows of the enchanters are burned
And their hearts are rusted with tobacco

The trees stretch out their teats
The mamey's flesh of well-baked brick
The tiny cinnamon-dusted breasts
Of nispero: cool sherbets in the sun

The valley on her knees before her males
Raises the high plumed palms
It's sugar-cane whose stalks erect
Are spurting out the dynamite of peace

But these palms with doric columns
Already build the future temple
Which public wisdom will inhabit
And a pure procession surround

In the deserts gnawed by famine
All these emperors these bootblacks
Will plant the pineapple and the eggplant
And pave the highroad for the savior

But the proud silence of the savannas
Is calling up the wrath of monsoons
The Central Bird is designing the arcanas
Of becoming and of expiation

[Translated by LOUISE BOGAN AND PAUL GOODMAN]

Drawing by Eugene Berman

JEAN SANS TERRE
AT THE FINAL PORT

To Claire Sans Lune

(First Version)

Landless John on a keelless boat
Having sailed many oceans without shore
A dawnless day at a townless port
Knocks with his boneless hand at a houseless door

He knows this woman without face who combs
Her faded hair across a silverless mirror
The restless bed the fireless embrace
That fear at dawn of evening's early terror

And on the wharves where ancient silence rots
And weary suns, too early picked, grow worse
The sea-gulls all their patience gone
Head for another universe

What joy or pain the longshoremen unload
Imported cradles or exported biers
Casks without oil or fabrics without wool
They whistle vainly sad tunes on the piers

These hides will never sole a shoe
This cotton never clothe the naked
This wood will never give off sparks
This wheat to holy bread be baked

What is this port at which none lands?
Where is this cape without a continent?
Which is this beacon without pity?
Who is this traveller without chastisement?

[*Translated by* WILLIAM CARLOS WILLIAMS]

JEAN SANS TERRE
AT THE FINAL PORT

To Claire Sans Lune

(Second Version)

John Landless in a ship without a keel
Having voyaged the horizonless seas
Docks a dawnless day at the cityless port
And knocks on some doors which have no houses

He knows that woman who has no face
In the mirrorless wall combing her hair
That bed without sheets that murmurless kiss
That love which is easy and lacks despair

In the shadowless square there is no fence
To stop his cutting from the roseless vine
The rose without petals to give to the girl
Of a song which will never be sung again

What is this boulevard without gods for sale ?
This twilight which blood does not begrime?
This green-grocery-store without grocery-men?
This clock countenancing the dying of time?

Why are these quays always without vessels?
These kegs wineless? These sacks riceless? These stocks
Without ginger, these bistros without dreams?
Only the sea is at work in these docks!

What is this port where ships never put in?
What is this dark and continentless cape?
What beacon is this, shining pitilessly?
And who is this traveller going scot-free?

[Translated by GALWAY KINNELL]

JEAN SANS TERRE
AT THE FINAL PORT

To Claire Sans Lune

(Third Version)

John Landless in a ship without a keel
The conqueror of oceans without shores
Docks in a townless port one dawnless day
And goes out knocking on the houseless doors

And well he knows that girl without a face
Combing her hair in the silverless glass
Her sheetless bed and her murmurless kiss
Her loving easy and tomorrowless

And recognizes galleys without oars
The mastless schooners and unsmoking stacks
Streets without bars and windows without whores
Nights without sleep and the unfearful docks

But past his brothers now he walks unknown
And does not see his sisters turning pale
Nor the grass trembling on his father's lawn
What is this city he does not recall?

There are no fences to the treeless park
To keep him from cutting the fount at the stem
And take it to the girl whose dreams were dark
Who hung herself for too much love of him

What street is this where gods cannot be bought?
What twilight where no lovers intertwine?
Where their own ashes put the streetlamps out
And clocks allow the perishing of time?

Why have they loaded these junks and tartans
With wineless wine-barrels and empty crates
Christs without crosses dancerless dances
Lemons without acid steel without weight?

Why on this wood is there no spark of fire
Why are these quays without a ship these stocks
Without customs these taverns without desire?
Only the sea is working these docks!

What is this port where no ship ever lands?
What is this cape that lacks a continent?
What is this phare in unmerciful hands?
What is this traveller wanting punishment?

[Translated by GALWAY KINNELL]

JEAN SANS TERRE
AT THE FINAL PORT

To Claire Sans Lune

(Fourth Version)

John Landless in a ship without a keel
Of horizonless seas the conqueror
Docks one dawnless day in the cityless port
And goes out knocking on a few houseless doors

He recognizes the faceless woman
In a glass without silver combing her hair
That sheetless bed those murmurless kisses
That easy and tomorrowless affair

But he passes unknown before his brothers
He does not see his young sisters pale-faced
The grass does not stir on his father's fields
What is this city with only one past?

Into the square without shadows over
The defenceless fence the stranger climbs
To pluck the unpetalled rose for the girl
Dead in his memory a dozen times

In the galleys the slaves without age
Unload wheat which has no gluten, wine
Lacking joy, the mirageless dreams
And that liberty which sings in vain

What is the use of these cranes which dig
Sometimes the sky sometimes the vessels
Loading cargos of ash unloading oils
Importing coffins exporting cradles?

179

Why are these quays without a ship? These barrels
Wineless? These sacks riceless? These stocks
Without customs? These bars, deliriums?
Nobody but the ocean works these docks!

What is this harbor where no ships puts in?
What is this headland dark and insular?
What is this beacon shining mercilessly?
Who is this unpunished traveller?

[Translated by GALWAY KINNELL]

JEAN SANS TERRE
AT THE FINAL PORT

To Claire Sans Lune

(Fifth Version)

John Landless sailing on a helmless boat
Through waveless oceans towards shoreless sands
Lands on a dawnless day at a townless port
Knocks at a houseless door with his boneless hands

Yet he remembers well these ancient galleys
These ageless slaves these steamless steamers
These barless streets these gazeless windows
These sleepless walls these godless dreamers

He knows this woman without faith and face
Who combs the curls of her fallen hair
He knows her restless bed her fireless embrace
Her love without desire and despair

He wonders why the cranes don't stop to load
Why they load caskets and the newborn grain
The wrathless lemons and the joyless wines
Why they load coal and unload ash again

This leather never will be shoe
This cotton never bandage the soldiers
This lumber will not heat the homeless
This wheat never feed the paupers

But who is he this nameless passenger
Who was not born and has no right to die
No reason to embark or disembark
But who is he this passenger without a lie?

[*Translated by* WILLIAM CARLOS WILLIAMS]

JEAN SANS TERRE
MOURNS FOR ONE DEAD

You were the beautiful
Machine of so much pleasure
Who held from knee to shoulder
Eternities of leisure

O sacred tower of vertebrae
Upon which was sung my name
The final chill already
Rises in you like shame

Faithless and cold already
Your body that has died
Lies hostile as a fortress
And I am left outside

And I who drank your glances
And I who fed your smiles
With such delirium
As floats from open vials

And I who took like sunlight
Your breath and warmth: alas
Scarcely can I remember
A few lilacs near grass

After the frights and sweating
The chills and the alarms
Your lips are lost to kisses
And love drains from your arms

After the crazy fever
Brought to your lips now shrunk
The broth of a pus which remembered
The nectar of kisses undrunk

For now you have forgotten
You do not know me now
And with calm eyelids lowered
Ignore my kiss and vow

You lie imperial
As on your forehead lies
The silence and as mutely
Destiny shields your eyes

Before your serene calm
Which shams the verity
Am I the unjust who
Contests eternity

Are you my adversary
Striving for my end
Can you abide my roving
More shameful than the wind?

Are you the Eumenide
Which persecutes my stillness
While your ovoidal eye
Broods over my blindness

Last night a chamber crowded
With dreams of light and sorrow
Now the cold shape of marble
That falls to earth tomorrow

Last night high and immortal
While I kept watch below
Your sentiment and senses
Are liquefied they flow

You are unloosed you wander
You drift beyond the straits
Beyond the darkened shoreline
Where one still shadow waits

And somewhere on earth
When things begin over
John Landless surely
Will be your pure lover

[*Translated by* CLARK MILLS]

JOHN SONLESS

The more of me there were
The lonelier I should be
After circumnavigation
There is no verity

I wished to seduce
I am without love
Already I sense
The vultures above

Harrowing the spaces
The meteor of black
Wishes his traces
Were a wide golden track

A wandering star
Of transient coal
It carves a smoky name
On the land-grant scroll

And its insane pyre
Of insipid crags
Doesn't even fire
The wind where it lags

I'll make no laws
I'll make no ties
Because my mouth
Too often lies

And I disperse myself
A shredded cloud
But with my shower
Descends a shroud

To the sand of Ur
From my very birth
Here ends my obscure
Trip upon earth

My final drop
That drills concrete
Will get absolution
For my wandering feet

This is infinity's
Vengeance and madness
I fall without offspring
Into full blindness

No son with black rimmed eyes
From too much grieving
Prostrates himself beside my grave
Casts shadows for my leaving

For the man alone
That glories demean
Can be no father
But Benedictine

Under my empty palm
No look of mine
When the hour of perfidy
Dictates my life-line

Deserted is my brow
Deserted is my knee
I resemble nothing
And I die within me

[Translated by ERIC SELLIN]

JEAN SANS TERRE'S
RIGHTS OF INHERITANCE

I am the only son of Solitude
And of Lord Oblivion who was Prince of Beaches
Knight of Foam and Admiral of Mists
Whose name is sung by every shell

After her husband's death my mother returned
To the granite land of her own family
Motionless upright on her cliff Chimera
She waits for the return of her mystic love

Orphan gathered in by the Sisters of Sorrow
Son of Oblivion and Solitude
Nourished a little both by flesh and dust
I set forth drawn by the tread of the longitudes

I have travelled through fields of the meadow-saffrons
The empire of lions and the federal states
Of olive and almond and through the republics
Of penguin and ox-fly; nothing was revealed

I am he who goes unknown through a field of clover
Indifferent to the date-palm that knew him as a child
Sometimes a dewy apple offers itself
I know: the fruit of the Tree of Knowledge lies

The creature is alone and the immovable angel
Ignores pity while dictating love
In the wind I am a whirl of sand
And I renounce in advance my hereditary rights

[Translated by Louise Bogan]

HERE LIES JEAN SANS TERRE

Now set me down
The whole length of me
Alongside of
The mystery

My four-doored heart
Where four winds wheel
With cold cement
And sadness seal

I weigh the shadow
Of trembling herbs
I tame the cry
Of unreal birds

But the songs in my throat
Are frozen dead
The desires of my feet
Do not leave my bed

Too poor the fare
In my life's hotel
Alas I am guilty
Of having not lived well

I strangled streams
For just one drop
I roasted peewits
In heaven's trap

I shook in orchards
The moons so much
I overturned casks
Of Saturn's scotch

My coffin falls
Falls and drowns
Among the ruins
Of irascible dawns

I'm no longer father
I am no longer son
My bright jaws smile
At new mysteries won

[Translated by LIONEL ABEL]

JEAN SANS TERRE
DEFINED BY YVAN GOLL

Landless John is the man who removes his shoes
When he touches ground, better to feel it:
Its feminine sand and its angry rock
And the essence of its different clays

Landless John is the man whom you have met
At the Marché aux Poissons
Haggling over two sous for a kilo of dawn
Carrying trout like an armful of roses

Touching the beef and the pear near the heart
And the carp in his stillness
Feeling the material of things of the earth
Estimating the material of clouds

The arch-ancient man: all plays on words
All hands he shook are dead leaves
All the girls have kept his touch on their necks
Like a gust of almond-scented wind

In the morning his head bore the reed basket of sorrel
And at evening the tiara of seven wisdoms
His curls were wilder than David's
However his polished skull will roll on the boneyard

Landless John walks the roads leaving nowhere
He walks to escape his shadow which binds him to the soil
He wants to possess nothing on this earth. Will he
—By singing—get free of his shadow, his other I?

[*Translated by* GALWAY KINNELL]

190